THE TURNBULL *Gamble*

WAYNE ERRINGTON AND PETER VAN ONSELEN

MELBOURNE UNIVERSITY PRESS
An imprint of Melbourne University Publishing Limited
Level 1, 715 Swanston Street, Carlton, Victoria 3053, Australia
mup-info@unimelb.edu.au
www.mup.com.au

First published 2016
Text © Wayne Errington and Peter van Onselen, 2016
Design and typography © Melbourne University Publishing Limited, 2016

This book is copyright. Apart from any use permitted under the *Copyright Act 1968* and subsequent amendments, no part may be reproduced, stored in a retrieval system or transmitted by any means or process whatsoever without the prior written permission of the publishers.

Every attempt has been made to locate the copyright holders for material quoted in this book. Any person or organisation that may have been overlooked or misattributed may contact the publisher.

Cover design by Philip Campbell Design
Typeset by Sonya Murphy, Typeskill
Printed in Australia by McPherson's Printing Group

National Library of Australia Cataloguing-in-Publication entry

Errington, Wayne, author.
The Turnbull gamble/Wayne Errington; Peter van Onselen.

9780522870732 (paperback)
9780522870749 (ebook)

Turnbull, Malcolm, 1954–
Liberal Party of Australia.
Prime ministers—Australia.
Political leadership—Australia.
Australia—Politics and government—21st century.

van Onselen, Peter, author.

324.0994

CONTENTS

PROLOGUE

Malcolm Turnbull was a happy man. Before winning the party-room vote for the leadership of the Liberal Party, he strode confidently down the corridors of Parliament House surrounded by the men, and they were all men, who were about to install him into the leadership. Peter Hendy, Wyatt Roy, Arthur Sinodinos, Mitch Fifield, Scott Ryan and Mal Brough would all be rewarded with promotions in the Turnbull ministry.[1]

Fast-forward to election night 2016. This time Turnbull was surrounded by his family at his harbourside mansion in Sydney's Point Piper. Brough hadn't lasted six months as a minister and didn't recontest his seat after a controversial exit. It was clear on election night that Hendy's 'bellwether' seat of Eden-Monaro had gone back to Labor. Roy had to wait nearly two weeks before delivering a classy concession: that he would have time for 'just being 26'. As Turnbull surveyed the wreckage around him, friends had to persuade him to make any sort of election-night appearance. The Liberals' federal director Tony Nutt and pollster Mark Textor were with Turnbull, both men frantically trying to confirm whether postal votes would help the Coalition secure a majority. Turnbull wanted to be able to say as much when he fronted the cameras; hence the long wait.

Election-night speeches usually have an audience of millions, although perhaps not by the time Turnbull got to his feet. It was after midnight when he finally took to the podium at Sydney's Wentworth Hotel, and his remarks were not directed to the public who had ridden the roller-coaster of the election count over six hours in lounge rooms and pubs. Turnbull's message was for a much smaller audience—Liberal Party MPs and senators who held his fate in their hands. Turnbull got caught up in the moment, his emotions leading him to ignore the speech his staff had scripted for him, which Nutt and Textor had approved. It was Turnbull unplugged, speaking from the heart. But his heart was black, courtesy of Labor's scare campaign on Medicare.

When seats are lost it's customary to wish the fallen well. To thank them for their efforts. Turnbull failed to offer such tributes even though he had worked so closely with some of the losers. The set speech contained the necessary words, but Turnbull was off-script. The missing words were a sign that he was not a fully evolved creature of the Liberal Party. John Howard, on the night he lost government and his own seat in 2007, had singled out Mal Brough, who had lost his seat in the Ruddslide. This was instinctive for a career politician like Howard. Not so for Turnbull. We all become somewhat consumed by our own mortality in tough times, but political leaders must rise above their own difficult circumstances.

It's also customary for the leader to take responsibility for the election result. This too was in the scripted speech never delivered. Turnbull, though, tried to deflect blame for the result to Labor's 'systematic, well-funded lies'. It was reminiscent of his speech on the night that the republic referendum failed in 1999, when he declared John Howard had broken the nation's heart. He looked rattled. Throughout his life he had dealt with failure by blaming everyone but himself and moving on to the next challenge. Yet in both of his efforts as Liberal Party leader, Turnbull's own mistakes largely explain his failures. Bad Malcolm was back.

INTRODUCTION

ON THE NIGHT the Liberal Party voted to depose Tony Abbott from the position of Prime Minister of Australia, one sign of the Turnbull camp's confidence was its media strategy. Abbott loyalists desperately visited all the television networks, which had gathered around Parliament House when the coup was announced, singing the praises of their man. Team Turnbull did little other than booking Senator Arthur Sinodinos on *7.30*. One issue on *7.30* host Leigh Sales' mind was whether Turnbull had changed since his last stint as leader had ended disastrously in 2009. She asked how the party could unite behind Turnbull. This question had also exercised the minds of the leaders of the coup and the MPs worried about their jobs, given the poor standing of their government under Abbott. 'Malcolm has promised to have a more consultative style, to reach out to people,' Sinodinos argued.

> He's had now virtually six years to reflect on the weaknesses and drawbacks of his first period of leadership, just like John Howard did when he lost in '89 and came back to the leadership in '95.

> Leaders reflect. They understand the messages from their first term as leaders and they try again.

Given the scale of his previous failure as leader, Turnbull would have had to have changed a lot to salvage the wreckage of the Coalition government.

Replacing even an unpopular prime minister was a gamble just a year from an election. Did Turnbull underwhelm so many observers because expectations were too high, or was his chief backer Sinodinos wrong when he claimed Turnbull had learned from past failures and re-emerged a new man, like John Howard had in 1995? Perhaps the gamble was doomed from the beginning—a public angry at Abbott's lies may have been unwilling to take his successor on trust. The positive public response to Abbott's removal suggests that voters were relieved when he was gone, even if the costs of change were yet to sink in. The costs of removing a first-term prime minister can be papered over for only so long, and resentment among some conservatives soon emerged. Turnbull discovered that he had taken over a party without a battle plan for the looming election, with little or no money set aside to fight a campaign. The unions were always going to strongly support a Labor Party led by one of their own, Bill Shorten.

The Turnbull gamble had one requirement for success—winning the 2016 election. Had the Coalition won as a minority government, as many predicted on the evening of the count, the gamble would have come under much more criticism. The final result, holding government with a small majority of seats that could disappear due to death or misadventure, may only delay the reckoning for Turnbull and those who installed him. The term 'Pyrrhic victory' refers to two battles against the Romans during the Pyrrhic Wars thousands of years ago. King Pyrrhus suffered such casualties that, according to Plutarch, 'one other such victory would utterly undo him'. This may turn out to be Turnbull's predicament following his victory on 2 July 2016. A huge loss of seats, greater dependence on the National Party, a Senate worse, perhaps, than the one that came before it, a feral conservative commentariat still furious about Abbott's removal, and divisions and distrust in sections of the parliamentary ranks. This is the outcome of the 2016 election, including the return of Pauline Hanson's One Nation—the antithesis of Turnbull's metropolitan liberalism. At times in the weeks following the election we needed reminding that Turnbull did in fact win, giving him a chance to prove himself as a prime minister with a public mandate for his prime ministership, if not for far-reaching policy reform.

The line between success and failure can be a fine one. Prior to the results being known at the July election, most commentators believed that the government would win comfortably despite an untidy campaign. Close national polls had been overshadowed by marginal seat–specific polling, which suggested that Labor couldn't win enough seats to prevail. It was the distance between this expectation and the perception at the end of election-night counting that the result was too close to call that led some to question the wisdom of the leadership change. Never mind just how depressed the Coalition's vote had been according to the polls when Abbott was prime minister.

The government took 90 seats into the election, but retained only 76. Had Turnbull won as many seats as Rudd in 2007—83—it would have been hard to argue that the result was in any way a failure. The tighter result leaves the question of whether or not the Turnbull gamble paid off a more contested one. But Turnbull won only four seats less than John Howard in 1998, and, unlike Howard in that election, Turnbull secured a majority of the popular vote. The better quality of the 'sandbagging' of seats—or making specific promises to electorates under threat—in 1998 raises legitimate questions about the ground campaign under Turnbull's watch.

This book analyses two different sorts of political gamble. The first is the decision of the Liberal Party to change leaders during the first term of a government for the only time in its seventy-year history. Had Turnbull overcome past failings that helped cripple his first time at the top in opposition? Did Turnbull surround himself with the right people? Had the divisions in the Liberal Party—inevitable after knocking off a first-term PM—been adequately thought through?

The second gamble was the long mid-winter campaign leading into a double-dissolution election. Labor surprised the Coalition with its scare campaign on Medicare. But problems set in much earlier than the campaign proper. The campaign is built on the perceptions of leaders and policies in place over a long period of time. The rudderless debates over tax reform, an aborted attempt to reform the federation, and the constant sniping from Abbott loyalists all marked out a slow and steady decline in the polls from their honeymoon pre-Christmas highs. Voters craved stability, which is why Turnbull's first instinct was to run full term. This saw him miss his window to take advantage of public approval of the leadership change—something Leader of the House, Minister Christopher Pyne, was urging him to do. Kevin Rudd's decision not to hold an early election when the Liberal leadership had last swung between Abbott and Turnbull cost him his prime ministership. Turnbull's decision didn't cost him his job but it did prevent the sort of thumping election victory that bestows authority on a Coalition prime minister. Having initially decided to go full term, why did Turnbull then choose to risk a long campaign for a mid-year double-dissolution election?

Prime ministers get a lot of advice. Some MPs hound them while others stay quiet because they don't want to be a bother. This can leave a busy PM listening to those he should not and missing out on the worthwhile advice of more polite MPs. This phenomenon didn't fully explain the double-dissolution election decision, but it did contribute to stumbles along the way. The PM must craft the team around him properly to ensure all valuable opinions are heard, not simply the loudest. Team Turnbull was too young and too inexperienced to do this.

Chapter One considers two of the flaws that hampered Turnbull during his first period of Liberal Party leadership in 2008–09, analysing whether Turnbull Mark II was really a changed man. Turnbull's temperament had been a major problem for him in his initial stint, and one that not all of his new band of supporters were certain he had yet mastered. Turnbull's first attempt at political leadership displayed similar mistakes to those of Tony Abbott—failure to listen, anger and poor judgement, compounded by condescension towards his colleagues both in private and occasionally in public. A central part of Turnbull's first-time leadership woes was the personality of the man himself. But he seemed conscious of these perceptions of his nature, telling *7.30*'s Leigh Sales a week after the coup, 'If you can survive setbacks ... you can come out of that sort of reforged, regalvanised as a wiser, better person.'

Since so many potential supporters had their doubts about Turnbull, they needed promises of promotion or policy guarantees to close the deal. These are all part of the inevitable costs—within the parliament and the community—of ousting a serving prime minister. Julia Gillard's costs included the loss of her 'golden girl' status, replaced by the image of an untrustworthy deputy-cum-leader. Turnbull appeared to overcome such antics, but they may have contributed to his timidity in policy terms, which then left expectations unmet.

Chapter Two concludes the survey of Turnbull's first experience of party leadership by analysing his policy positions and the way he lost his job in 2009. Climate-change policy will continue to play an important role in Australian politics for the foreseeable future and Turnbull's position remains unsatisfactory. We consider the gulf between the beliefs of any given Liberal Party leader and the compromises forced upon them by the constraints of party, parliament and electorate. Turnbull came to office in unusual circumstances. Whatever his personal beliefs, he was always going to disappoint those who were hoping for Abbott's policies to recede into the distance.

Chapter Three shows the reality of governing a divided nation through a divided government. Turnbull's management of his government in the lead-up to the election was just as damaging as the institutional constraints on him, even as he worked hard to be more consultative than Abbott had been. Tax reforms were floated and sunk in succession. Turnbull showed little interest in a more liberal approach to asylum-seekers, wasn't prepared to step back from a public vote on same-sex marriage, and remained wedded to the Abbott approach on climate change. Some of this was inevitable, even necessary, but Turnbull's own rhetoric contributed to raising expectations of a different path. An agile start gave way to a quagmire of problems; all the while critics further to the right toasted each and every misstep, magnifying the significance of these with their microphones.

Chapter Four introduces these delusional conservatives (delcons). With election telecasts dissecting the close result on 2 July 2016, the floodgates of criticism and retribution quickly (and prematurely) opened. The delcons called for Turnbull's head, for the return of Abbott and many other bizarre demands. But while the Coalition was bruised, the delcons' numbers are much larger in the opinion media—most notably News Corp tabloid columnist Andrew Bolt—than in the parliament. Even Eric Abetz and Kevin Andrews moderated their language in public, though less so when backgrounding journalists or talking to colleagues. Beyond Abetz, Andrews, Abbott and perhaps new MP and apprentice delcon Andrew Hastie, it's hard to find anyone else in parliament who fits this extreme category. The chapter discusses Abbott's behaviour before and during the campaign, shows how Turnbull handled the inevitable sniping and offers some thoughts on the likely conservative–liberal divide in the years ahead.

Chapter Five shows the preparations for the July poll—final policy manoeuvres before an early budget, and legislation to change the Senate electoral system and trigger an early poll. The hastily pulled together Senate reforms, so the brains trust around Turnbull thought, required a double-dissolution election to 'clean out' the crossbenchers unhappy with reforms designed to put them all out of a job. But timing an early election with a double-dissolution trigger left Turnbull needing to call for an eight-and-a-half-week campaign rather than the usual four-week campaign, to get the house and the Senate in alignment. If you count from when he flagged such a campaign would occur, which for all intents and purposes marked the beginning of the campaign, the length was over ten weeks. Not since 1969 had a campaign lasted this long. Between four and five weeks is the norm. Further, dissolving the entire Senate at once halved the quota of votes required for a seat and made it easier for minor parties to succeed. The trigger, defeated legislation to resurrect the Howard-era union-busting Australian Building and Construction Commission, didn't resonate as an issue in the campaign. The government's response to the trade union royal commission wasn't even released before polling day, as had been promised.[1]

The July election meant going to the polls straight after the budget, not giving the government time to sell its key measures or, as in the case of winding back superannuation taxation concessions for high-income earners, for example, tweak them to avoid a backlash. And don't forget it had to bring forward the budget by a week due to the timing of the election, the handling of which exposed fractures in the relationship between Turnbull and his new treasurer, Scott Morrison. Conservative critics, including the delcons, jumped on the perception, if not the reality, of tensions between a prime minister and his treasurer. It was all very messy.

Chapter Six analyses the first half of the election campaign. The woes on the government's side contrasted sharply with a Labor campaign that used modern techniques, reacted quickly to problems as they developed, and was well resourced with good ads and even better scare campaigns. Somehow, even as the polls drifted away from Labor shortly after Turnbull took over, Bill Shorten maintained unity and Labor ground its way back into the contest. But the party still only secured its second-worst primary vote in its history. In contrast, the government was returned with a majority for the first time since 2004—a sign, perhaps, that the problems Turnbull encountered were as much about an unforgiving public mood towards incumbents as any failure on the campaign trail.

While Turnbull performed poorly in the televised debates, those events did not play as central a role in the 2016 campaign as they had in earlier battles.[2] A bigger problem was that the hand-picked federal director, Tony Nutt, appeared out of touch with modern campaign techniques and too cautious about sharing research so it could best be used to shift results in the government's favour. Mark Textor remains the best pollster in the business, but his strategy of largely staying positive needed to be buttressed by attack ads, the likes of which he so successfully oversaw in 2004 against Mark Latham. Labor certainly expected ads akin to the L-plate Latham ads, having tested them within its own focus groups in a bid to learn how to diminish their effectiveness. Labor found that it had no way of combating them, which is why the opposition was so joyous when they never materialised.

Those close to the Liberal campaign claimed that they were left with little money, preparation or prospects by the Abbott regime. Turnbull ended up needing to make a hefty personal donation late in the campaign. But what about the eight months between when Turnbull took over and the election was called? Abbott's administration can wear only so much of the blame. And if what was taken over was so bad, why go to the polls earlier than necessary, and with a longer than usual—and therefore more costly—campaign? We wrestle with these questions in this chapter.

Chapter Seven focuses on why Labor's 'Mediscare' strategy proved so successful. After the advertising blackout, when little could be done to change the trend, Liberal campaign headquarters research showed that undecided voters were not breaking towards the Coalition. The reason was Labor's Medicare scare campaign—a powerful exercise in misleading the electorate about Coalition intentions to privatise public health, but one built on legitimate fears in the community that the conservatives were eroding the principle of affordable and universal healthcare. Use of the word 'conservative' is deliberate, for it was the Abbott-led Liberals who had contributed to this perception with their attempt to introduce a co-payment for GP services. Notwithstanding his massive preferred-prime-minister lead over Shorten, Turnbull could not overcome the distrust engendered among voters by cuts to health spending—which Abbott had guaranteed not to pursue on the eve of the 2013 election. The savvy Labor scare campaign exposed this trust deficit.

Chapter Eight takes us back to election night, and bizarre scenes of Labor happily losing the election while the Coalition winners bickered about who was responsible for lost seats. The National Party had the most reason to be happy, once again improving its position against the odds. We look at the challenges facing Turnbull in a new parliament, including the fact that he has presided over a fall in the number of Coalition women in parliament—not something he would have anticipated when taking over from Abbott. We conclude that the Turnbull gamble on the part of the Liberal Party was worth the inevitable costs, a judgement shared by a majority of the party room. Turnbull's own gamble on the timing of the election, however, and his failure to articulate a vision that was compelling to a majority of Australians, meant that his prime ministership had been disappointing to many.

One

TRANSACTION COSTS: PAST AND PRESENT

AN IMPORTANT GROUP of Liberal MPs had made up their minds about the relative merits of Tony Abbott and Malcolm Turnbull as leaders and election winners by the end of 2014. They worked over the following months to convince the likes of deputy Liberal leader Julie Bishop, other cabinet ministers and wavering back-benchers that Abbott had to go. Young Queensland MP Wyatt Roy, in particular, was disillusioned by his direct dealings with Abbott and travelled around the country to convince colleagues that the government was heading towards a historic first-term loss. NSW MP Peter Hendy, who had only entered parliament in 2013, was another who wanted to remove Abbott but was far from convinced that Turnbull was the right replacement. This unlikely group of moderates and conservatives had plenty of time to think about what such a change would mean for the government and the wider Liberal Party. The more senior figures working for a change of leader had seen opposition leaders come and go. They had seen their counterparts in the Labor Party destroy two prime ministers and muttered that it would never happen in the Liberal Party. They thought about the costs of leadership change. Could the party be unified if Abbott had to be blasted out by a prolonged campaign of destabilisation? Could the party be reunified? What if Abbott, like Kevin Rudd, chose to stay around and return the favour? What if Bad Malcolm hadn't really changed?

Two years after the moves to change prime ministers began, we know more about the stakes of the Liberal Party's Turnbull gamble. As we have seen, for some of the coup organisers, the potential costs and benefits were very personal, with parliamentary seats and ministerial positions at stake. For Turnbull, one of the decisive factors in regaining the leadership was disillusioned Abbott supporters deciding to back Turnbull despite being less than impressed by his leadership in 2008–09. But a core of less conservative MPs and senators drifted into Turnbull's orbit more naturally. One of the costs for Turnbull would come in promoting supporters whose skills he didn't rate or who came with problems he would inevitably have to deal with as prime minister. Mal Brough had been up to his gills in the effort to build a case against former Speaker Peter Slipper through information provided by Slipper's staffer James Ashby.[1] Owing Brough favours for his support was one of Turnbull's more expensive transactions. Giving Brough the honour of special minister of state was a deft touch. Nobody knew what the position was about so he wouldn't be missed if he was forced to step down. Arthur Sinodinos came with baggage as well. One of the reasons he became alienated from Abbott was the poor handling of Sinodinos's status in the ministry while he faced the Independent Commission Against Corruption inquiry in New South Wales in 2014.

Victorian senator Mitch Fifield had been one of the three shadow parliamentary secretaries who expedited the removal of Turnbull in 2009 by resigning his frontbench position.[2] Scott Ryan is a powerful factional figure from Victoria who describes himself as a 'dry'—or free-market Liberal—and let us know in no uncertain terms the error in our book *Battleground*, which described him as a 'moderate', duly corrected for the second edition. As senators, Fifield and Ryan were personally less dependent on the performance of the parliamentary leader than were House of Representatives members.

However, they so despaired about the quality of government under Abbott that both men accompanied Turnbull on his walk into the party room for the September 2015 vote and were rewarded for their efforts. Yet both Victorians had to overcome doubts about Turnbull's leadership style, having witnessed his arrogance and poor political judgement. Indeed, Ryan couldn't stand Turnbull at first. He felt that Turnbull didn't understand the Liberal Party, and he was concerned about the way Turnbull had handled the debate over an emissions trading scheme (ETS) as leader in 2009. Fifield had been talked down to by Turnbull in a way that few politicians' egos would allow them to ever recover from. Ryan wanted guarantees about Turnbull's handling of climate change—both in terms of policy and consultation about any changes. While he was uncertain about whether Turnbull had truly changed, though, he was certain that Turnbull would perform better than Abbott. As a party loyalist first and foremost (as senators tend to be), Ryan wasn't impressed by Abbott's tactics during the same-sex marriage debate, when he used the National Party to dilute support for a conscience vote. For Ryan, the gamble on Turnbull was worth it.

The decisive votes within the wider parliamentary party came from MPs and senators historically doubtful about Turnbull's suitability to lead the Liberal Party. Michaelia Cash, a minister from Western Australia, is a close ally of conservative factional leader Mathias Cormann, yet two weeks before the coup she went to see Julie Bishop to let her know Abbott had lost her support and Turnbull would do as a competent alternative. And the spearhead of Turnbull's strategic push to oust Abbott was Arthur Sinodinos, John Howard's long-time chief of staff, who could never be accused of being a dripping wet moderate. Senators James McGrath and Simon Birmingham joined with Ryan in counting numbers in the weeks leading up to the September challenge. New lower-house MP Craig Laundy was important as a conduit to marginal-seat MPs, including members of the 'class of 2013' who owed their seats to Abbott's victory, helping judge the timing as to when their survival insticts would come to the fore.

Sections of the conservative wing of the party had long complained that when Abbott seized the leadership from Turnbull he retained moderate faces in the inner circle—such as Christopher Pyne as Manager of Opposition Business and then as Leader of the House, and George Brandis in a Senate leadership role. Both have become part of Turnbull's leadership group. A party's platform does not change simply because of a hard-fought leadership contest. The contrast between recent Australian changes of prime minister and Theresa May's uncontested accession to the UK Conservative Party leadership, and therefore the prime ministership, after the Brexit vote in 2016, is interesting. May used her power to choose her ministry to clear out supporters of the previous leader, David Cameron, who was certain to shuffle off the stage. A closely fought contest with a leader determined to linger in the parliament comes with much higher costs. Turnbull needed supporters, and after his failed first term as leader, he couldn't afford to be fussy about where they came from.

Bad Malcolm

Malcolm Bligh Turnbull's middle name represents a family tradition of paying tribute to William Bligh, whom an ancestor of Turnbull's had supported when Bligh's controversial leadership style got him into trouble as Governor of New South Wales. In contrast to Bligh, who after suffering a mutiny as captain of the *Bounty* seemed to learn nothing about leadership, Turnbull would have to improve his leadership skills to succeed the second time around. After working with him the first time he was leader, senior party figures had three main concerns about a Turnbull comeback: that he lacked political judgement, had a poor temperament and was out of touch with core Liberal Party values. Similar doubts had plagued Turnbull's first two runs for the leadership. He had long been regarded within the party as a difficult personality to deal with.

Just as it would in Turnbull's case, a combination of leadership style and policy substance brought down opposition leader

Dr Brendan Nelson in 2008. Nelson had defeated Turnbull for the job by three votes after the 2007 election loss. Distancing himself too quickly from Howard in the week after the election loss cost Turnbull the leadership back then. Nelson was aware that the leader's role after an election loss was to heal the party, but he took consultation and consensus to absurd levels when developing a climate-change policy. That Nelson was finished after just a year was clear enough. Observers, though, wondered why Turnbull would challenge again for the job so early in what could be a lengthy period for the Liberals in opposition. Surely he should bide his time and let Nelson absorb the blows of an ascendant prime minister, Kevin Rudd, and his government. Such opinions misunderstand the nature of political leadership. The fact that an experienced cabinet minister was struggling as opposition leader meant little to Turnbull. Natural leaders have confidence in their ability to beat the odds. Former treasurer Peter Costello learned the wrong lesson from the Liberal leadership wars unfolding around him during the 1980s. He believed that the Liberal Party needed orderly succession to avoid returning to the bloody conflict between John Howard and Andrew Peacock. What heals divisions in the Liberal Party, though, is a strong and successful leader—a status that comes only after multiple election victories.

Turnbull had no doubt that he was destined to be such a leader. He never bided his time, not even during his relatively long stint between leading the Liberal Party. While still at university, he was already well into his career in journalism, covering the NSW parliament for the leftist newspaper *Nation Review*, the Catholic Church–owned 2SM, and Kerry Packer's Channel Nine, or as Turnbull put it, serving 'Marx, God and Mammon'.[3] His precociousness made Turnbull a natural leader in many spheres—head prefect at Sydney Grammar School, winner of the prestigious Lawrence Campbell Oratory Competition and Rhodes Scholar for New South Wales. Musician Steve Kilbey competed with Turnbull as a high-school debater, remembering Turnbull as 'the Muhammad Ali of high-school debating. The total heavyweight champ. It almost wasn't fair! He was like some big kid of 14 playing football with the Under 7s.'[4] In time Turnbull would head up the Australian Republican Movement and become the managing director of Goldman Sachs Australia. Midnight Oil drummer Rob Hirst was a year behind Turnbull at high school. He remembered a 'plummy brew of eloquence, imperiousness and un-humble pie, plus a kind of sighing, saturnine resignation that his job necessarily involves being constantly surrounded by cretins'.[5] Despite being on the board of the university union, Turnbull didn't spend enough time on campus to play a big role in university politics. He therefore missed out on an apprenticeship that has helped many Australian political leaders learn their trade. Political leadership is quite different from leadership in other spheres. Success requires the skills, and the moxie, to think that you can make decisions that affect millions of people. The tenure of an Australian political leader, though, relies on maintaining good relations with a relatively small number of colleagues. Kevin Rudd had problems in both these realms. However confident Turnbull might be at decision-making, it would be worth little if colleagues were not impressed with his personal style. In private conversation, Turnbull struggled to show interest in what his colleagues had to say. An intellectual gadfly, he was easily distracted without always realising the rudeness of his behaviour. Colleagues joked to each other that often a phone conversation with Turnbull would end abruptly, and before he had even hung up he could be heard starting his next conversation with wife Lucy, daughter Daisy or whoever was next in line for his attention.

Turnbull is fascinated by how systems and people work, and often shows this in his interactions with the public. He has learned to feign interest in what voters are up to when he doesn't find them interesting. A bigger test for his leadership was how he would treat his supposed equals in cabinet, let alone a humble backbencher. When it came to dealings with his colleagues, the barrister in Turnbull made him a forensic listener rather than an empathetic one. Privately Turnbull has often lamented the limits of the Westminster system, which forces a prime minister to choose his executive from the gene pool available in parliament. Naturally, such confidences have largely been directed at parliamentarians who share his business background.

The Full Nelson

Ancient history is its own discipline in the humanities, but unfortunately in modern politics, relatively recent events are too soon categorised as such, given observers' focus on the here and now. The return of Turnbull as Liberal leader in September 2015, with the added responsibility of being prime minister less than one year out from the next election, was always going to carry significant costs. Bad blood internally, as well as perhaps the impression of chaos in the eyes of the electorate. And the loss of a powerful criticism of Bill Shorten's hand in two coups against prime ministers. But potentially the biggest cost was the re-exposure of leadership failures Turnbull suffered from during his first stint as leader. Had he changed his style? Had he learned from past mistakes? The rise of Turnbull to the leadership in 2008, alongside his downfall at the hands of Tony Abbott one year later, gives us a yardstick by which to judge the latest Turnbull gamble.

Always being the smartest guy in the room and having the wrong temperament to suffer fools can be a disastrous combination for a political leader. During Turnbull's first leadership stint, colleagues complained that he would cut people off or lecture them in the party room. Former Howard minister Wilson Tuckey foreshadowed a motion to require secret ballots in the party room to decide policy positions. Cockiness and wishful thinking from Turnbull supporters didn't help. 'When Nelson's leadership terminated,' an anonymous frontbencher boasted, 'the influence of a lot of the old Howard brigade was terminated too. Nick Minchin's no longer a player in Canberra. Eric Abetz too. Chris Ellison left. There's a clear sense that the Howard era is over and we're now moving on.' Minchin, Turnbull would learn, was far from finished.

The vagaries of opposition can be illustrated by the fact that the Liberal and National parties took a unified position on climate change to the 2007 election, a position over which they fought continually for the next two years, at the cost of two Liberal leaders. As environment minister under Howard in 2007, Turnbull had helped to develop the government's emissions trading policy. To win the leadership, Nelson had courted his party's greenhouse sceptics, arguing that Australia should have no scheme at all unless there was an international agreement that included developing countries. Turnbull tried to paper over the differences, helpfully explaining to journalists that he and Nelson both supported Coalition policy. Former cabinet ministers Nick Minchin, Kevin Andrews and Tony Abbott, plus most National Party MPs, publicly backed Australia waiting for global action while the official Coalition spokesman, Greg Hunt, was barely noticeable in his support for Turnbull and the policy that had recently been confirmed by the shadow cabinet. Inevitably, these policy differences became the focus of leadership speculation, given Nelson's poor polling. Nelson's lack of political judgement was undermining his support from the very right-wingers he was trying to court with his rhetoric on an ETS. The opposition seemed determined to make a spectacle of itself and let the government off the hook without having to explain the detail of its own policy. While opinion polls favoured Rudd's position on the ETS, the public knew little about how such a scheme would work. The prospect of increased power and petrol bills without commitments from the leading global polluters to adopt a similar scheme would later be the basis for an effective scare campaign.

Nelson was widely viewed as a nice guy unable to 'cut through', a term often used about Labor's Simon Crean when he faced Howard at the peak of his popularity. A few Nelson loyalists argued that he should be given some 'clear air' to prove himself once Costello, an ominous presence who had declined to take the leadership after the 2007 loss, had quit parliament, whenever that might be. Opposition leaders, though, are never given clear air. Another helpful colleague preferred an injection of something other than oxygen, telling journalist Laurie Oakes, 'It's going to be like putting your dying family dog to sleep. Brendan is dying. The sooner we put him to sleep the better.' Turnbull knew that he would be on the wrong end of this sort of backgrounding as soon as he took over the leadership. He rationalised his position, though, because he had little respect for Nelson's political talent and didn't mind telling Nelson this. He knew he would make a much better fist of the job. Nelson surprised everybody by declaring the leadership vacant at a hastily organised party-room meeting in September 2008. Nelson lectured colleagues about disloyalty and told them he wouldn't be contacting them individually to seek their votes. He again offered up the proposition of taking on the government more aggressively over climate-change policy. The meeting lasted only half an hour. Not for the first time, a Liberal leader was preparing to sacrifice himself to the cult members.

Turnbull had only arrived in Canberra from Italy that morning. His wife, Lucy, was commissioner for the Australian pavilion at the Venice Biennale of Architecture. Treasurer Wayne Swan quipped that Turnbull was returning from Venice with his 'Andrew Peacock tan'. Turnbull's office found out about Nelson's party-room meeting along with other MPs when a fax arrived in his office. Having already assumed too much about the voting intentions of Liberal MPs once, he wasn't about to repeat his mistake. On his laptop, Turnbull had a spreadsheet that divided Liberal MPs into three groups: those pledged to him, to Nelson, and those undecided. A jet-lagged Turnbull telephoned most of his colleagues, bar a handful of Nelson's closest supporters, pointing towards his greater popularity in head-to-head polls with Nelson, a theme he would return to when making a third tilt at the leadership, against a different leader and in government. Could they really picture Brendan Nelson winning an election? Turnbull exuded passion for the job. Victorians Mitch Fifield and Tony Smith, however, abandoned Turnbull over climate-change policy, and publicly announced their intentions in order to give the impression of momentum in Nelson's favour. The leader of the 'anyone but Malcolm' faction was Nick Minchin. Minchin's and

Turnbull's experience of the Liberal Party could hardly have been more different. Minchin had held positions in the party organisation since 1977. After one ill-fated run for pre-selection in the 1980s, Turnbull's party involvement only recommenced when he became the Menzies Research Centre chairman in 2001. The Liberal Party was set to replace a man who had been an ALP member in the 1980s, Nelson, with one who had worked closely with former ALP figures such as Neville Wran and Nicholas Whitlam in the 1990s. To party traditionalists, the trend was not good.

Abbott, Bronwyn Bishop and Concetta Fierravanti-Wells, all from New South Wales, shifted towards Turnbull. Bishop's vote was met with Turnbull sacking her from the shadow ministry. Young right-winger Alex Hawke helped recruit fellow Sydneysiders, with some on the right upset at Nelson's efforts to reform pre-selection processes. The Victorians, too, were split, with Costello's long-time friend Michael Kroger unable to back Nelson, not that he personally had a vote in the party room. A dozen Costello supporters backed Turnbull.

Both his supporters and detractors knew that Turnbull would be no ordinary political leader. Turnbull's enormous self-confidence and his contempt for Nelson led him to believe that a capable opposition could unmask Rudd as the shallow political operator that Coalition MPs believed him to be. He impressed business leaders and Liberal members who saw him perform at fundraisers, but the public had known Turnbull for twenty years and never warmed to his imperious style. Some compared Turnbull to Mark Latham, brilliant but inclined towards narcissism and anger. One even suggested that Turnbull was a combination of Latham and another failed opposition leader, the Liberals' John Hewson. A lifetime of activity on the fringes of national politics seemed to have taught Turnbull little about the art of politics. Turnbull laughed off Kerry O'Brien's attempts to get him to discuss his short temper on *The 7.30 Report*.

Malcolm Turnbull became the twelfth leader of the federal parliamentary Liberal Party on 16 September 2008. Considering that some Liberal leaders have lasted for months rather than years, this relatively small number of leaders bears out the fact that the party both expects and rewards strong leadership. Certain traits are essential to being a strong leader, of course: Turnbull had the requisite intelligence, ambition, self-confidence and high-handed demeanour. Authority in the Liberal Party, though, comes not from a victory in the leadership contest, however wide the margin. It can only derive from uniting the disparate interests, personalities and factions of the party. An election victory, of course, can turn the rugged individualists on the conservative side of politics into slavish followers. From opposition, unity takes consultation, inspiration and, most of all, patience. Turnbull had shown none of this latter quality in his political or earlier careers.

Speaking without notes to his first party-room meeting as leader, Turnbull tried to find common ground with his Liberal colleagues. He had been unimpressed with Nelson's speech to the party room after their contest the previous year, when he was considerate enough to tell Nelson that he would need to toughen up. Turnbull now told the party room he was humbled to be elected leader of this great party. He would work hard to unite the party. He shared its values: opportunity, fairness, enterprise, energy. The fact that so many profiles of Turnbull opened with the fact that he was the wealthiest Member of Parliament irked him. He couldn't change his past but he could change the way he dealt with people. 'We will be a united, a cohesive team,' he later told reporters. He evoked his father. 'I know what it is like to be very short of money,' he said. 'I know what it is like to live in rented flats. I know what it is like to grow up with a single parent, with no support other than a devoted and loyal father.' The reference to rented flats was typical of Turnbull's inability to hit quite the right note. In Turnbull's defence, the Double Bay rental market can be brutal.

On the same day, Queenslander Barnaby Joyce pushed aside the little-known Territorian Nigel Scullion as leader of the National Party in the Senate. The job itself was not so influential, but the fact that the Nationals would place in a leadership position someone well known for criticising Coalition policy was a sign of just how difficult a task Turnbull would have in uniting the opposition. Joyce was no longer a maverick. His populism was now the dominant view inside the Nationals.

Turnbull provoked laughter from the government benches and journalistic scribbling about his 'ego issues' when he quoted himself in Question Time. On a lighter note, he wasn't sure whether Sydney's AFL team was the Swans or the Roosters. Newspoll had mixed results for Turnbull. The public thought he was strong and decisive, but less trustworthy and caring than Rudd or Nelson. Perceptions of arrogance were also going to be a problem.

While Turnbull developed his leadership persona and perhaps some policies, Rudd kept the new opposition leader busy responding to announcements. The prime minister was determined to occupy what Tony Blair called 'the radical centre', a mythical place with lots of activity but not much achievement. The radical centre, though, does have the virtue of throwing up lots of policies and plans for the opposition to bicker over.

By December, Rudd's lead over Turnbull as preferred prime minister was similar to that he had enjoyed over Nelson before the leadership spill. The two-party preferred polling was predictably disastrous at 59–41. The anonymous carping began. Responding to criticism of his policy and leadership style, Turnbull was scathing. 'I don't place any store on anonymous smart-arses who make comments like that. If they don't have the guts to put their name to it, then I am not going to waste time worrying about what they have said,' he told 2UE. Twelve months earlier, when the anonymous smart-arses were his supporters undermining Nelson, Turnbull had been silent on the issue. He was already learning about the costs of changing political leaders.

Dr Nelson's Diagnosis

Upon announcing his retirement from parliament, Nelson had a parting shot for Turnbull. 'I'm not vindictive,' he told *The Sydney Morning Herald*'s Peter Hartcher. 'I don't lie awake at night with a chip on my shoulder. But he's a person who wants to tempt you in that direction ... If you had any idea of what he said to me over those ten months [of Nelson's leadership], you would be shocked.' Then came the diagnosis:

> He's got narcissistic personality disorder. He says the most appalling things and can't understand why people get upset. He has no empathy ... At first, I thought he was demonstrative, demanding, emotional and narcissistic, using his wealth and charm for seduction, and always with a sinister threat just beneath the surface.

Nelson reflected on the story Turnbull had related to Hartcher's colleague Annabel Crabb about Packer threatening to have Turnbull killed and Turnbull returning the threat. 'At first, I didn't think it was that bad. But it is.' As Hartcher pointed out, the definition of narcissistic personality disorder contained in the American Psychiatric Association's *Diagnostic and Statistical Manual of Mental Disorders* could describe any number of politicians. Diagnosis required five or more of the following traits:

1. has a grandiose sense of self-importance
2. is preoccupied with fantasies of unlimited success, power, brilliance
3. believes that he or she is special and unique and can only be understood by, or should associate with, other special or high-status people (or institutions)
4. requests excessive admiration
5. has a sense of entitlement
6. is interpersonally exploitative
7. lacks empathy
8. is envious of others or believes that others are envious of him or her
9. shows arrogant, haughty behaviours or attitudes.[6]

Maybe Turnbull was nine for nine, but that doesn't prove the disorder. Nelson's diagnosis was influenced by his being in the way of Turnbull's ambition. Profiles of Turnbull contain many brickbats from former associates and adversaries. While they all, like Nelson, have an axe to grind, it is the sheer number of Turnbull's alienated acquaintances that impresses.[7] There are also those, however, who know him well, faults and all, and hold him in the highest regard. The notion of disorder, always controversial in psychology, is a tendency taken to an extreme. Even a high level of narcissism doesn't necessarily indicate a pathology. Or, as Crabb put it in Turnbull's case, there is an important distinction between egoism and egomania.

All children are narcissistic. Most of us grow out of it. A parent absent during childhood, something Turnbull shares with Rudd, often holds the key for those who retain narcissistic traits. Turnbull's mother, Coral Lansbury, who left her husband and son to pursue an academic career in the United States when Turnbull was nine, corresponded with him by exchanging audio cassettes. Lansbury fed his ambition and taught him about politics. As Turnbull has said publicly many times, 'I missed her terribly … I was very close to her and it was heartbreaking when she left.' The young Turnbull was self-aware, writing, 'One has to be somewhat egotistic to achieve anything, given the jealous, carping nature of the mass of humanity.'[8]

The founder of psychoanalysis, Sigmund Freud, saw the potential for narcissism to drive political leadership. Australian political history is replete with narcissistic personalities, some of whom became successful prime ministers.[9] A study of American presidents found that those thought to have the characteristics of 'grandiose narcissism' were disproportionately found among presidents considered by scholars to be 'great'. However, such men also dominated the ranks of presidents impeached by Congress.[10] Successful leaders back their judgement for better or ill.

This notion of advantages and disadvantages of attributes such as self-confidence goes wider than narcissism. Our conclusion about Tony Abbott in *Battleground* was that Abbott lacked the self-awareness to learn from his mistakes: he didn't see himself as others saw him—ironic given his Jesuit schooling, which encourages such reflection. The danger in changing from Abbott to Turnbull was that while the public would find the change in tone disorienting, the style of leadership would be the same. The two men were more similar than either would care to admit. James McGrath and Mal Brough had concerns but were prepared to take the risk. Equally so the likes of Mitch Fifield and Scott Ryan. Arthur Sinodinos was more confident that Turnbull had changed.

The qualities that make some politicians stand out as leaders are difficult to define. Electing a parliamentary leader is often an act of faith. The very qualities that make for great leaders contain the seeds of disaffection and disappointment. Self-confidence becomes narcissism, audacity can with hindsight look like recklessness. Political scientist Graham Little, who also wrote about the 'strong leadership' styles of Ronald Reagan, Margaret Thatcher and Malcolm Fraser, differentiated between Bob Hawke's vanity and Paul Keating's pride to show that narcissism can produce quite different types of leaders. Hawke courted the people's love. Keating wanted to make it on his own: the people could take him or leave him.[11]

When does a narcissistic personality stop being a prerequisite for political power and start becoming a problem? Point seven above—lack of empathy—holds the key, as Nelson pointed out. Turnbull knew that he would be dependent on others in order to prosper in politics and was willing to cultivate relationships in the parliamentary party. He just wasn't very good at it. As things started to go wrong, admirers in the party and the media thought it inevitable that someone as smart, capable and determined as Turnbull would soon master the art of political leadership. Should they really have been surprised, though, that the essence of Turnbull's personality did not change? He could be charming in short bursts, and was impressive in interacting with all manner of people as he wandered about the country with Lucy. He showed a genuine interest in the rich diversity of people who pop up on the campaign trail. But those who interacted with him more regularly without wife Lucy present, such as his party colleagues and journalists, as well as any number of people in business circles and the republican movement, had inevitably experienced Bad Malcolm as well.

Unlike Hawke, Turnbull doesn't always expect to be loved by his colleagues or the public. Although not above bouts of populism, Turnbull has more of Keating's pride than Hawke's vanity. At the same time as Nelson was offering his diagnosis, Turnbull was disengaging from the electorate that should have mattered to him most at that point—the party room—and planning to do what he thought was right on climate change. His willingness in 2015 to bury differences over climate-change policy when searching for votes in the party room to depose Abbott indicated a more mature politician. Six years to reflect on his weaknesses; six years to become desperate enough to compromise his beliefs; six years to learn how to suffer fools.

Turnbull's 'crash or crash through' style of 2009 has been compared to Gough Whitlam's. Yet before Whitlam employed those tactics against a hostile Senate, he was one of the most successful opposition leaders in Australian history, painstakingly working to reform the Labor Party and its platform over almost six years. Tellingly, Whitlam was the last opposition leader to hold that position for any substantial period prior to being elected prime minister before Tony Abbott came close to matching his achievement. Without the legal threats that were a feature of his business career, Turnbull simply wasn't very persuasive. Opposition leader is a frustrating role. Prime ministers have resources and patronage to complement their powers of persuasion. Fewer stories circulated about Bad Malcolm when he became prime minister, but that could change under the pressure of two finely balanced houses of parliament.[12]

Judgement

Tony Abbott called them 'captain's calls': the times when a leader makes decisions without the normal consultation with colleagues that inevitably requires compromise and second-best solutions. As Abbott found, though, there is more scope for captain's calls in opposition than in government. Abbott's first captain's call in opposition was to impose an expensive family leave policy on a sceptical Coalition. In government, he couldn't deliver it. As opposition leader in 2008–09, Turnbull wasn't positioning the Coalition for a two-election return to government. He wanted to win in 2010. This ambition led to some hasty decisions. Jumping at a news story alleging that Treasury Secretary Ken Henry had advised Rudd against an unlimited bank deposit guarantee when the global financial crisis hit, Turnbull was embarrassed when Henry flatly denied the story. Characteristically, Turnbull was unable to admit during a lengthy Kerry O'Brien interrogation on *The 7.30 Report* that he had simply made a mistake. Turnbull had allowed the government to turn Henry's warning about the implementation of the guarantee (one justified by its troubled early days) into an attack on the opposition leader's judgement.

Turnbull's lack of judgement was exemplified by Utegate, which he stumbled into just as he was beginning to match Rudd in the economic policy debate. Turnbull's incessant rhetoric about Labor's budget profligacy obliged the Coalition to identify at least a few billion dollars in savings, especially since its main contribution to budgeting in the previous year had been to add to the deficit by holding up a tax rise on alcopops. Turnbull proposed an increase in tobacco excise instead of changes to private health insurance. This ultimatum was the highlight of a strong 2009 budget reply speech: 'a tough choice for a weak prime minister'. For the first time in a while, opposition backbenchers were smiling behind their leader. As a bonus, Rudd's spin merchants had leaked the details of all the big-ticket items in the budget ahead of time, giving Turnbull a rare opportunity to make the political running in budget week. Arguing in favour of a tax hike on cigarettes made the alcopops obstructionism look a little silly, so that bill was quietly allowed to pass. After eighteen months of complaining about opposition negativity, the Labor government was still lacking a double-dissolution trigger.

Despite trying to link Rudd to a number of minor scandals since becoming leader, Turnbull had barely dented the confidence of his opposite number. Godwin Grech, a political knave with a name from central casting, was the principal adviser in Treasury's financial systems division. He was the senior official in charge of a $250-million government-sponsored finance program for car dealers known as OzCar. He was well known to senior figures on both sides of politics. Late in 2008, Grech had rejected a chance to move from Treasury since he thought that was where he could be of most use to 'MT and the party'.[13] Grech approached Turnbull with suggested questions about OzCar for a Senate estimates hearing, and for Turnbull to ask in Question Time. Turnbull's decision to put so much faith in Grech makes sense only if Grech was the reliable source of damaging leaks such as the documents on the ill-fated FuelWatch scheme and the bank deposit guarantee, as Labor later alleged. Yet, if a senior public servant is regularly leaking documents to the opposition, his integrity is not exactly beyond reproach.

John Grant, owner of a car dealership in Ipswich, west of Brisbane, had long made available a vehicle for Rudd's use in his electorate, where Grant lived. Rudd declared the ute, its registration and insurance on his list of pecuniary interests. Grech explained to a Senate committee that Swan had made representations on behalf of Grant's application to OzCar. Other MPs had done the same on behalf of constituents. Turnbull soon had the unequivocal denials from Rudd and Swan that he would use against the prime minister and treasurer. Grech suggested that a Senate inquiry into the OzCar legislation would be the best forum. Email correspondence later released by Turnbull shows Grech identifying with the Coalition, referring to how 'we will be silly not to allow the Bill through'.[14]

Grech showed Senator Eric Abetz and Turnbull an email that proved Rudd's office had contacted Treasury about Grant. Abetz was later defended by colleagues who claimed that he warned Turnbull to concentrate the attack on Swan. Other members of the leadership team were becoming frustrated at the secrecy surrounding what Turnbull and his chief of staff Chris Kenny were cooking up with OzCar. Turnbull could have let the media make the running. Howard had always kept the dirt-digging of the likes of Abbott at arms-length. But Turnbull was at the centre of it, thoroughly enjoying the spadework. He clashed with Rudd's economic adviser, Andrew Charlton, telling him not to lie for his boss. 'This whole OzCar issue will be very damaging for you,' Charlton recalled Turnbull telling him. 'Integrity is the most important thing in a man's career ... You know and I know there is documentary evidence that you have lied.' It was a boastful performance, at best tying Turnbull to the events before the Senate committee, at worst alerting Rudd's office to what was to come. Either way, it lacked judgement. Journalist Steve Lewis asked Grech about correspondence between the Prime Minister's Office (PMO) and the treasurer. The leak was timed to set the stage for Grech's appearance before a Senate committee. Grech later claimed that he denied to Lewis the existence of the email. The government had already announced that a search of PMO and Treasury computers failed to turn up any such correspondence. This should have meant something to Turnbull, the OzEmail pioneer. Charlton denied having heard of Grant before his name came up in parliament. For Turnbull, though, the clear denials were only proof of a cover-up. Months of cautious probing of government weaknesses had left him frustrated.

Correspondence between the Treasury and the treasurer's office on Grant's application was revealed to the Senate Economics Legislation Committee. Eric Abetz led the opposition's questioning of Grech. The level of interest shown by Swan's office in Grant's application was evidence enough for a substantial attack on the government. 'I certainly had the impression that he was not your average constituent,' Grech remarked. Barnaby Joyce chipped in, 'I can smell burning flesh.' Swan, who had assured parliament that Grant received no special treatment, had a lot to answer for. Turnbull's complaints about the accountability of the myriad schemes set up to deal with the financial crisis were at last vindicated, but the Coalition wanted more.

Later in his questioning of Grech, Abetz quoted from a document purportedly from the PMO to Treasury about the Grant claim. Only later was the significance of Abetz's role in leading

Grech's testimony realised. Sensing the importance of the occasion, government senators attempted to interrupt proceedings, making it appear as though they were protecting Grech from Coalition bullying. Grech played the perfect awkward, disinterested public servant, tearful at having the information dragged out of him. When finally allowed to respond, the length of Grech's answer would have done Sir Humphrey Appleby proud. Eventually, Grech challenged Rudd's flat denial that his office had made representations for Grant. 'It was certainly my understanding that the original representation with respect to Mr Grant came from the Prime Minister's Office,' Grech told the committee, qualifying his claim by referring to his imperfect memory.

Turnbull called on Rudd and Swan both to resign. 'This is a shocking abuse of power and a betrayal of public trust,' he told parliament. The affair earned the grungy yet grand title of 'Utegate'. Rudd upped the ante by bringing in the Australian Federal Police and calling on Turnbull to cooperate with the investigation into what the government was now confident was a concocted email. Turnbull claimed not to have a copy, the first public sign that his call for Rudd's resignation had been hasty. Meanwhile, the claims against Rudd let Swan avoid the very serious questions about his responsibility in Utegate. Back on the front foot, Rudd blitzed the electronic media with calls for Turnbull to produce evidence to back his allegations or resign. 'This entire email is false, it is fake, it is a forgery,' he told Channel Nine. Turnbull wasn't backing down, criticising Labor senators for their treatment of Grech. In parliament, all attacks on Swan were turned into attacks on Turnbull. Leader of the House Anthony Albanese gave a foretaste of what a Rudd–Turnbull election campaign might look like with attacks on Turnbull's business career.

While this was going on, AFP officers were raiding Grech's house. Grech, who had been hospitalised in February 2009, was coping poorly with the attention. Police reported that the fraudulent email had been sent from Treasury to Grech's personal email account. After this news reached parliament, Turnbull wasn't around to finish Question Time. 'If an email has been concocted or fabricated, it's been concocted in the Treasury ... That's Mr Swan's responsibility, not mine,' he said later. Turnbull's call for a judicial inquiry looked a little hollow when the Coalition voted with Family First senator Steve Fielding to block a Senate inquiry into Utegate, just the second time in history that a referral to a privileges committee had been voted down. If Turnbull was experiencing what for him would have been a rare case of self-doubt, he wasn't showing it during an extended interview with Kerry O'Brien. It was an unfortunate day for Turnbull's office to be attempting some image-softening courtesy of an appearance on ABC's *Australian Story*. The cameras captured the office in full panic mode.

Reporters were quick to seize on any links between Turnbull and Grech. One of Turnbull's former economic advisers, Paul Lindwall, had once worked with Grech at Treasury. Grech had worked briefly for Joe Hockey during the Howard government as a departmental liaison officer. The AFP widened its investigation to include leaked documents from the entire period of the Rudd government. Turnbull was learning the costs of putting too much faith in one source.

Turnbull continued to distance the opposition from the fake email. 'We had no reason to believe that Mr Grech was not telling absolutely the truth,' he said. 'He's a very senior Treasury official, a person in whom the Government, Mr Rudd and Mr Swan have placed considerable trust. So we were entitled to rely on what he said.' Turnbull admitted that he had spoken to Grech on numerous occasions in recent months, knowing that the AFP were about to discover as much. He tried to concentrate minds in the party room by pointing out that Rudd would easily win an early election, but couldn't prevent disbelieving backbenchers venting about their leader's parliamentary tactics.

Turnbull had played into every criticism made of him by suspicious colleagues, from impatience to arrogance to naivety. Knowing the rewards that would come to him if he could damage Rudd's leadership, he had been prepared to take a risk on Grech's credibility.

Taking risks in business had brought Turnbull enormous rewards. As Annabel Crabb wrote, 'The bigger, richer, riskier prize has always held a special enchantment for him.' Along with his many successes in business, Turnbull has had his share of duds. In business, though, failure is just an experience to learn from. In politics, and in the Liberal Party in particular, failure takes years to live down. Turnbull knew this. While opinion poll results in the wake of the scandals that regularly consume Canberra can be counter-intuitive—sometimes the public simply isn't interested in day-to-day politics—the public didn't miss Utegate. They were less concerned about any personality defects the affair might have revealed in the opposition leader than the bare fact of his incompetence. Turnbull suffered the biggest single drop in the approval rating for an opposition leader in the twenty-five-year history of Newspoll. Three different polling organisations found that Coalition gains of recent months had disappeared. MPs travelling home to their electorates confirmed the surly public mood. Speculation about how long Turnbull could last as leader began even though there was still no obvious challenger. The undermining came from conservatives including Tony Abbott. This pair had a long and often fractious history, with so much more to come.

The AFP ultimately cleared the opposition leader of any involvement in the Utegate email. Repeatedly asked at a press conference whether he could have handled the affair any better, Turnbull could only promise, 'I will reflect on it ... I guess every politician regularly makes errors of judgement.' Having already had six weeks to reflect, this was as close to admitting his mistakes as Turnbull could bring himself. Under pressure from the Senate privileges committee, Abetz apologised to the prime minister. From the hospital bed where he was being treated for depression and other illnesses, Grech claimed that his faked email was based on a real one that could not be located. He said that he provided the contents of the email to the Coalition only under duress. In response, Turnbull released emails that showed Grech taking an active role in the plotting, requesting the fateful 12 June meeting with Turnbull and Abetz.

Two of the potential costs of electing Turnbull as Liberal leader in 2015, then, would be his temperament and his judgement. If Turnbull hadn't learned from experience there wasn't much the rest of the government could do about these vices. By comparison with Abbott, whose 'captain's calls' had made the government a figure of fun, and given the lack of serious alternatives, the party was prepared to take the gamble. There was one area of leadership, though, that those around Turnbull could influence. Most policy decisions are not captain's calls but the result of deliberation by the leadership team, the cabinet and the party room. Turnbull was both more socially and economically liberal than most of those who installed him into power. To win the leadership, he promised consultation, and given the favours he owed, he would have to provide it. Whatever Turnbull's favoured positions on same-sex marriage, immigration and climate change, his options would be limited.

Two
THE BOWER BIRD

Bowerbirds don't discriminate when hunting for objects to add to their bowers, displaying natural treasures like fresh flowers, feathers, and cicada wings alongside objects like ballpoint pen lids and bottlecaps. Competition for bower decorations is fierce, and male bowerbirds will steal desirable trinkets from other bowers to improve their own.

—American Natural History Museum

DESPAIRING AT THE tepid nature of the 2016 election campaign, *The Australian*'s Canberra bureau chief Phillip Hudson had a solution for Malcolm Turnbull's plummeting approval ratings. In the vein of the *West Wing* episode 'Let Bartlett Be Bartlett', Hudson thought that the Liberal Party should 'Let Malcolm Be Malcolm'. Just as *The West Wing* was a fantasy of what a liberal American presidency could look like, the idea of Turnbull unbound appealing to the Australian electorate was an indulgence for many Australians in the months after Abbott was deposed. Turnbull had been in the public eye for so long, and Abbott's prime ministership had been so turbulent, we were free to project onto the new leader our nation's hopes. He would set his party straight on climate change. He really only sabotaged the National Broadband Network on Abbott's instructions, and now he would fix it. His heart wasn't in the same-sex marriage plebiscite, so let's get on and legislate it immediately, with Turnbull leading the debate. His business networks would turn the economy around. And he'd get around to the republic stuff eventually.

Which Malcolm Turnbull were we entitled to expect as prime minister, though? The free-speech advocate who successfully defended the publication of *Spycatcher* in the 1980s? The bipartisan leader of the republican movement? The far-right policy wonk who spouted supply-side nonsense about tax cuts paying for themselves from the government backbench? The conviction politician who said he didn't want to lead a party that wasn't as committed to action on climate change as he was? Turnbull was all of these things yet none of them as prime minister. He'd already had a number of careers, never spending more than a few years at each. This combination of ambition and restlessness required intelligence and adaptability. The remarkable thing about Turnbull's CV is the breadth of his interests. Politics was something Turnbull had only dabbled in until 2004, contributing to the image many in the Liberal Party hold of him as a dilettante. Even after he committed to a parliamentary career, his eclecticism made him like a bower bird, collecting shiny objects to show off to others. Turnbull drove then-treasurer Peter Costello spare with his 279 income tax–cut proposals as a novice MP. In his memoir, Costello accused Turnbull of finding new ways to spend money as Minister for the Environment. Prior to entering parliament, Turnbull chaired the Menzies Research Centre, which under his direction produced any number of policy innovations that got Turnbull noticed but didn't impress the Howard government.

Turnbull's political career, though, has been punctuated by bold declarations of his beliefs. The best guide to Turnbull's ideology is his first period of leadership in 2008–09 when, perhaps unwisely, he fought hard for his beliefs against economic stimulus during the financial crisis, and for action on climate change. The result was rapidly falling popularity and an agonising defeat to, of all people, Tony Abbott—a self-described policy 'weather vane' on these issues.

A liberal Liberal

Since the first iteration of the Liberal Party shortly after federation, right-of-centre Australian political parties have been united as much by what they oppose as by any set of ideas. Opposing socialism brought together the Free Traders and the Protectionists in 1909, because the emerging Labor Party was seen as the greater of evils. A large part of the success of Robert Menzies in founding the Liberal Party in 1944, prior to the end of World War II, was to redirect that focus to appeal to the so-called forgotten people—the middle class. This appeal was aimed at overcoming perceptions that the party's predecessor, the United Australia Party, was too close to big business. Menzies was the beneficiary of what Liberals opposed far more so than what they collectively represented. Liberals rejected communism and, with that, Labor's brand of socialism. It was an easy political kill for Menzies during the heady days of the Cold War.

Long after Menzies departed politics, and with Gough Whitlam and Bob Hawke dragging Labor to the centre, opposition to socialism only got the party so far. Members were calling for a positive agenda to reflect the times. The dries were a collection of radical free-market thinkers who wanted to free the economy and, in particular, the industrial relations system. The economic philosophy of the dries wasn't electorally popular, and support for it at the top of the Liberal Party, including during both periods of Howard's leadership, was patchy. Howard engaged in enough privatisation and union-bashing to give his government a sense of direction, but on tax and spending in the second half of his government's time in office, Howard wasn't prepared to go beyond the limits of electoral competition.

Abbott's two years as prime minister in 2013–15 suffered from the same lack of readiness for office as Malcolm Fraser's government of 1975–83—inadequate renewal of personnel, and a failure to step back from the political combat of previous years and evaluate which policies the party should keep or discard. The single-mindedness of Abbott's pursuit of power was a different ethos to the traditional conservative reasoning behind seeking office—to keep Labor off the treasury benches. For Abbott it was about attaining power for power's sake. The goal was to constantly tear Labor down, not simply when policy failings were present. Unlike in the 1980s when the Liberals selectively opposed and supported policies on merit, Abbott's mantra was to make life as difficult as possible for Labor—'we can't govern from opposition' was his line to colleagues. Abbott found it hard to break from the negative mind-set once in power. The question now is to what extent will a Turnbull-led Liberal Party transform for the modern political era? At one level, the need to do so is diminished because of the lack of introspection Labor has undergone in recent times. Failure to reflect seems to be a bipartisan problem in the body politic. The Liberal Party, within our entrenched two-party system, is organisationally resistant to behaving as 'Labor-lite', as conservatives dismissively portray the inclination to occupy the centre ground. Abbott was representative of a more ideological approach to politics than that of Menzies' generation. This tendency began with the shift to free-market solutions to growing inflation and unemployment in the 1970s. It has been galvanised by the importation of American-style cultural politics, whereby conservatives seek the votes of blue-collar workers on the basis of social rather than economic policy.

The support Turnbull was able to muster for his challenge to Abbott was cobbled together in response to deficiencies in Abbott's leadership style, and the choice of Turnbull was simply because he was the most viable alternative candidate. Climate change aside, he wasn't conspicuous in dissenting from the policies that got the government into trouble, most notably in the 2014 budget with its cuts to welfare, deregulation of university fees and Medicare co-payment. Turnbull's personal polling numbers, perceived political charisma and name recognition in the electorate put him ahead of alternatives such as Julie Bishop and Scott

Morrison. The fact that Turnbull had a more moderate pedigree than either of these candidates was a mere coincidence.

The Liberal Party has for most of its existence been more pragmatic than ideological, seeking to retain power as a primary goal. But what does doing so offer progressives or liberal economic reformers? Or indeed social liberals? Even Howard, who was unashamedly socially conservative, would not have tolerated governing for its own sake, as was apparent from his final-term push for further industrial relations reform in the shape of WorkChoices. While the conservatives undoubtedly entrenched their power base within the Liberal Party during the dominant leadership of Howard, it was hard to know what they sought to achieve beyond maintaining incumbency.

Nine days after winning the Liberal Party leadership in 2008, Turnbull took on TV host Tony Jones and his audience on the ABC's interactive *Q&A* without the cover of other panellists. He owned up to smoking pot as a young man, but admonished himself for having done so. He couldn't quite nail down the number of houses he owned—a memory loss that Labor frontbencher David Feeney came to understand during the 2016 election campaign. Most importantly, though, the program gave Turnbull the opportunity to provide more depth to his background and beliefs. He talked about the strength of his father. Clumsy as Turnbull's attempts to deflect Labor attacks on his wealth may have been, he was right to point out that he didn't have an easy start in life. Given the departure of his mother, the writer Coral Lansbury (descendant of a British Labour Party leader), when Turnbull was just nine, he thus shared with many political leaders, including Howard and Rudd, the loss of a parent at a formative age. He paid tribute to his father for never having a bad thing to say about his mother.

Supporters portray Turnbull's liberal views as more in touch with the founding traditions of the Liberal Party than Howard's conservatism. Attorney-General George Brandis, for example, has written about such things many times.[1] Yet, the *Q&A* interview was one of the few occasions when Turnbull went beyond his primary tasks of attacking the government and discussing specific policies. He was reluctant to be drawn into potentially divisive discussions of political philosophy before his leadership was consolidated. He made it clear, though, that he wanted new policies. 'We can't run in 2010 on policies of 2007 and 2004,' he said. As prime minister he has sought to rhetorically line up such thinking with words like 'agility' and 'innovation'.

As chair of the Menzies Research Centre shortly before entering parliament, Turnbull was happy to be associated with a range of innovative policies on tax, housing and education. For example, Christopher Joye, later a columnist at the *Australian Financial Review*, was commissioned to write a paper on the viability of reverse mortgage loans, which Turnbull proudly took to Howard for consideration. It went nowhere. When he became leader of the parliamentary party in opposition, Turnbull was disappointed to find how many constraints were placed on him by colleagues. To placate conservatives, he appointed one of their own, Kevin Andrews, to head a policy review. The new leader was committed to retaining Nelson's highest profile (but expensive) promises—boosting the aged pension and blocking a number of revenue measures in the Senate. Turnbull had argued against cutting fuel excise by five cents, which would cost $2 billion annually, prior to Nelson's budget reply speech, and it was speculated that he had leaked that fact in order to embarrass his leader. He quickly dumped Nelson's idea. Falling petrol prices eventually made the issue less salient. Like Kevin Rudd later on, Turnbull didn't want to be distracted from the central concerns of the electorate by talk of a republic. He declared there would be no republic as long as Elizabeth II reigned. The urgency of renovating Australia's constitution was now dependent on the quality of Britain's National Health Service.

The Robert Menzies Lecture in October 2009 gave Turnbull another chance to outline a philosophy:

> Lucy and I have lived a life of enterprise all our lives: we have started businesses, employed people, taken risks, made

> investments and we have learned what so many politicians and bureaucrats forget, that the wealth of this country is founded on the tireless energy and optimism of millions of Australians having a go ... Resilience, optimism, energy, they are the essential elements of enterprise.[2]

Turnbull would have to look for votes outside the socially conservative blue-collar workers who helped Howard in 1996 and 2004. Another hurdle would come from the rank-and-file membership. More than a decade after Howard's first election win, this group was more socially conservative than the electorates Turnbull was hoping to win over. Speaking in support of a charity for families dealing with premature births, Lucy revealed that she had suffered two miscarriages in her late thirties, causing her and Malcolm to give up plans for a larger family. Turnbull had told Wentworth preselectors that his greatest regret was not having more children.

As shadow treasurer in 2008, Turnbull had been one of the few political leaders to defend Bill Henson's artistic freedom when a Sydney gallery was raided by police. Turnbull owned two of Henson's works. When Nelson joined Rudd in expressing distaste at Henson's work, Turnbull telephoned him to complain, pointing out the number of art galleries in Wentworth. As leader later that year, though, news that a Victorian school had contacted a prospective child model on Henson's behalf was too much for Turnbull. 'I share the outrage that has been expressed by many people at these events,' he said.

Labor's bill to grant equal rights to gay and lesbian couples with respect to superannuation and other areas of the law split the Coalition—a reminder that opposition to same-sex rights isn't limited to today's debate on marriage. South Australian senator Cory Bernardi blasted the bill as a 'pernicious form of social engineering'. Turnbull, whose electorate has the highest proportion of 'pink voters' in the country, gave Bernardi a dressing-down for speaking against settled party policy. More was to come as this relationship became toxic.

However contrived Rudd's use of Australian idiom appeared to be at times, he at least made the effort. Turnbull is Turnbull, take him or leave him. Voters seemed to decide before he even became leader that they would rather leave him. Labor's polling on Turnbull found that dislike of him centred on his personal style as much as his wealth. But this research faded into the background after Abbott assumed the Liberal leadership. Suddenly opponents of Abbott saw Turnbull as the perfect counterweight to a leader they had worried was too conservative even for the Liberal Party. This attitude, which seemed to be embedded in the wider views of the public according to the polls, catapulted Turnbull back into calculations as an alternative when Abbott's prime ministership started to falter. It artificially elevated Turnbull's promise and praise, because they were always paralleled to Abbott's. Once Abbott was, politically speaking, dead, buried and cremated, Turnbull started to be judged in isolation for the first time since his brief stint as opposition leader.

Stimulating Debate

While he made his first waves in Australian politics as a republican, and is famous for his social liberalism in a conservative party, it is in the economic sphere that Turnbull wants to make his mark. In the early months of the first phase of his leadership, Turnbull had communicated his passion for the environment, for ideas, for new technology, for Australian entrepreneurship. Turnbull's policy instincts were indeed for a free market, but his interest in renewable energy and innovation also made him lean towards government intervention.

At the onset of the 2008 financial crisis, when he was shadow treasurer, Turnbull was quick to point to the quality of banking supervision introduced under the Howard government. Rudd was proving quite the interventionist in government, quickly reacting to the crisis with a stimulus package and turning a $4 billion broadband package into a National Broadband Network, the cost of which is yet to be finalised. Recalling the lengths Rudd had gone to before the 2007 election to style himself as an economic conservative, Turnbull labelled Rudd a 'born-again socialist'. Their debate over economic philosophy in the press during the summer of 2008–09 set the stage for Rudd's announcement of a second, much bigger stimulus package. More cash handouts were accompanied by spending on schools, roads and other infrastructure. The opposition concentrated its attack on the big turnaround in the forecast budget projections, from a $20 billion surplus to a $20 billion deficit. Turnbull started to spruik the work of Stanford University economist Professor John Taylor, who argued that stimulus measures were only effective if they were permanent, not temporary. 'When you increase people's permanent income they are more likely to spend than if it is just a one-off hit, a one-off bonus, a windfall,' Turnbull explained. Turnbull had form when it came to grabbing hold of unorthodox economic thinking. His 2005 raft of 279 tax proposals was based on the assumption that lowering the top marginal tax rate would provide incentive and reward for effort, create jobs and therefore have a limited cost to the budget—the same rationale used for the company tax cuts in the 2016 budget. This magic-pudding approach to tax marks one of the big differences between conservative parties in Australia and the United States. Republican presidents Ronald Reagan and George W Bush introduced big tax cuts, leaving their successors with massive budget deficits. Howard and Costello were more cautious, conditioning the public to believe that while tax cuts were important, budget surpluses are always good policy.

Turnbull wanted to tap into that public suspicion of deficits to attack Rudd's economic policies. The Coalition's reputation for fiscal discipline—largely unwarranted, given the scale of the China boom on Howard's watch—was the only political capital at hand. With a round of tax cuts already legislated to come into effect in July 2008, bringing them forward was at least no more fiscally irresponsible than Howard and Rudd had been in promising them in the first place. Turnbull went on the attack in parliament. 'The plan we were presented with by the Prime Minister yesterday reeks of nothing more than panic,' he said. 'Somebody has to stand up for fiscal discipline.' He released a YouTube video reminding young Australians that they would be paying the bills. Opposing the package outright was a risk. His argument in favour of a more targeted stimulus would be drowned out by government claims of the opposition blocking funding to schools. Even with the knowledge we have now, that debt didn't reach the levels in the estimates, opposing the stimulus was a risk worth taking for Turnbull. While painfully aware of the downside, Liberals and Nationals from across the ideological spectrum could unite behind a strategy of opposing Labor's build-up of debt. Some may have had second thoughts as they watched South Australian senator Nick Xenophon extract a billion dollars in concessions for his crucial vote.

The part of the package that Turnbull criticised most was also the most popular with the public. 'Imagine if 60 years ago, Ben Chifley and Bob Menzies had sent everyone a cheque for £50 instead of building the Snowy Mountains scheme,' he said. He described Rudd's plans as Whitlamesque, as though a reference to a period when millions of voters weren't even born would be a killer political point. His line that the government was spending like Paris Hilton at least had the virtue of being contemporary. Turnbull's primary economic strategy was a little easier to understand. He ran around the country crying 'jobs, jobs, jobs' into any microphone he could find. Turnbull's 'Jobs for Australia' forums in regional areas, long before he began railing against three-word slogans, received lots of local attention but had little impact on the national debate. Turnbull's extensive travels to consult small business produced a policy that included various tax breaks and a provision to allow taxes on profits to be clawed back if losses were experienced in subsequent years. His case that the stimulus package was too big received no support from G20 leaders who backed each other's efforts at spending their way out of crisis.

The most common complaint Turnbull faced from within the Coalition was that the opposition would not benefit from being a pale imitation of the government. 'Let Labor govern, live with the consequences, and if they are adverse then we can undertake to rectify it when we return to government,' he told colleagues who wanted the Coalition to oppose Labor's changes to industrial relations more vigorously. Turnbull's problem was that some in the Coalition still thought that WorkChoices was a fine policy. The party-room debate featured an exchange between Turnbull and Costello, with Costello calling for a tougher line. When the government tabled its industrial relations legislation, Turnbull had no desire to resist. He emerged from a party-room meeting to declare, 'The Coalition accepts WorkChoices is dead; the Australian people have spoken.' This earned Turnbull his first public rebuke from Nelson, who urged his party to find a backbone.

The prospect of a budget deficit emerging if the government embarked on a second stimulus package provided risk and opportunity for the opposition. Turnbull's strategy on the crisis wasn't entirely negative. He was full of advice on things the government should be doing to strengthen the financial system. Turnbull knew US Treasury Secretary Hank Paulson from their days together at Goldman Sachs. He was, though, representative of a class of people whose ever more complex financial dealings had caused the crisis. Rudd was offering to put $10.4 billion in the bank accounts of welfare recipients while Turnbull argued in favour of bringing forward planned tax cuts. He also underlined the value of a permanent boost to the aged pension as a stimulus measure but supported the government's package. Detracting from the opposition's attempts to debate responses to the crisis was Turnbull's wealth. Days before redemptions from a property fund were frozen, affecting hundreds of thousands of people, Turnbull moved money out of the fund and into other investments. Turnbull was simply taking the advice of a financial adviser, but it was a distraction from one of his few promising lines of attack.

Losing It

Turnbull's first bout as Liberal Party leader ended, as it began, with divisions in the Coalition over climate change. Whatever happens to Turnbull's leadership into the future, it's hard to imagine the brutality of the ending matching what happened in late 2009. With a vote on Rudd's ETS legislation approaching, Turnbull tried to get the Coalition to adopt something approaching a coherent policy. Turnbull's public comments were ahead of the settled Coalition position, sparking the usual complaints from mostly anonymous detractors. The leader back-pedalled again. He no longer had the authority to lead. Liberal backbencher Wilson Tuckey emailed colleagues about Turnbull's 'arrogance and inexperience'. Tuckey's message was soon made public. 'I can think of no better issue [than climate change] upon which to fight an election be it early or on time,' Tuckey wrote from the luxury of one of the safest seats in the country, which he still found a way to lose to the Nationals at the 2010 election. It was easy enough to dismiss Tuckey (Joe Hockey likened him to the uncle who imbibes too much at the family wedding). Indeed, few Liberals shared Tuckey's 'bring it on' bravado. Instead, Turnbull's weakness in the polls was convincing waverers that the party faced a choice between losing on Rudd's terms and losing while fighting for a matter of principle.

Some reflection on why Rudd was the most popular prime minister in the modern era was called for. As with Howard, Rudd's partisanship was contained within substantial arguments over policy. Rudd's ties to Labor were no deeper than Turnbull's to the Liberals. The Coalition seemed determined to learn nothing from Rudd's ascendancy. Crying foul about Rudd's duplicity in styling himself an economic conservative prior to the election and a social democrat afterwards didn't resolve the problem that Turnbull had failed to style himself as much of anything.

The situation looked so bad for Turnbull that frontbenchers, including Andrew Robb, felt the need to offer their 'full support'. Robb was the preferred candidate of conservatives who thought an election under Turnbull's leadership would be a disaster and Robb's low-key style was the antidote. But if some old fogies in the party room wouldn't leave him alone, Turnbull at least showed some affinity with young voters on *Q&A*. Sharing the panel with the ever more impressive Julia Gillard, Turnbull enjoyed the interaction with a specially selected audience of people too young to care about Utegate.

Turnbull, Robb and environment spokesperson Greg Hunt faced the impossible task of negotiating with the government and their own backbench simultaneously. Sensing that Turnbull was unconcerned about parting ways with the National Party over the ETS, Joyce raised the stakes by declaring that a future Coalition government should repeal any ETS that it inherited.

Andrew Robb announced that he was stepping down from the frontbench to deal with depression. Former industry minister Ian Macfarlane had credibility among conservatives and so took over Robb's role in the negotiations. Macfarlane, though, quickly attracted flack for not being as consultative as Robb. Macfarlane admirably supported Turnbull to the bitter end.

Commentary marking the anniversary of his ascension to the leadership had concentrated on Turnbull's failure to articulate a vision. Of course, just what Rudd stood for was far from obvious, but the prime minister could stand behind government actions. Turnbull's problem was that opposition decision-making in response to Rudd's legislative agenda was with few exceptions messy, drawn-out and unnecessarily public.

Impressed by UK conservative leader David Cameron's advice not to let the left own the environment issue, and refreshed from his September break, Turnbull was in no mood for compromise. John Howard, too, had returned to Australia with steely resolve after meeting a British conservative leader in 1988, only to spark a debate on immigration that mortally wounded his leadership. Turnbull finally said publicly what he had long been saying privately. 'I will not lead a party that is not as committed to effective action on climate change as I am,' he declared. 'If the party room were to reject my recommendations to them that would obviously be a leadership issue. That's perfectly plain, quite clear, and I am asserting my leadership and my authority as the leader of the party,' he said, presciently. The backbenchers weren't quaking in fright, though. Some complaints were directed against Turnbull's chief of staff Chris Kenny's abrasive style, comparing him unfavourably with Howard's long-serving lieutenant Arthur Sinodinos.

Turnbull's thinking was the mirror image of the most implacable opponents to climate-change action. If he was going to lose the leadership or the election, he would do so on his own terms. This new strategy immediately ran into opposition. Backbenchers accused Turnbull of misrepresenting them when he claimed that he had 'the overwhelming support in the party room for the position we're taking on climate change'.

Even though Nelson's wobbliness on climate change had been so costly, Turnbull found himself adopting the position that Nelson had been advocating. 'Kevin Rudd is rushing in an emissions trading scheme for purely political grounds,' he claimed. Turnbull announced that he didn't want to vote on an ETS 'without knowing what the global community will agree to or not at the Copenhagen summit at the end of 2009 and without knowing what the new US president will do'. Throwing in the uncertainty of the financial crisis made delaying the legislation a respectable position provided the inevitable headlines about backflips and hypocrisy weren't too damaging. Business, though, was critical. Even those such as the Minerals Council, which wanted the ETS watered down, didn't want the uncertainty of delay.

The sense of crisis, though, would only buttress public support for the government. Opposition leaders usually look like they relish too much the prospect of economic doom. One of Rudd's communication successes was to normalise public use of the term 'global financial crisis' in order to ensure that blame for any recession stayed overseas and didn't attach to the government.

The Sydney Morning Herald's Phillip Coorey put the view of some Coalition backbenchers that 'not renowned for his patience or tolerance of lesser beings, Turnbull may be going out of his way to set the scene for a fiery exit by Christmas'. Turnbull's public position at this point was that the option of voting against the legislation was still open. Yet having the party leader repeatedly asked whether or not he would stay in the parliament if he lost the leadership was not building confidence. Joe Hockey had decided that he would take the leadership if it became vacant. Hockey and Turnbull fronted a joint press conference to calm the issue. On *The 7.30 Report*, Abbott conceded that three opposition leaders in one term was hardly unprecedented. Indeed, Howard and Rudd had both been the third leaders in a parliament prior to winning an election. Behind the scenes Abbott was more than agitating. He was sniping—increasingly so after being overlooked for Christopher Pyne for Manager of Opposition Business.

Turnbull called a party-room meeting on 17 October to debate the ETS amendments backed by shadow cabinet. Policy and politics became indistinguishable. Whatever Turnbull's ultimate views on climate-change policy, he couldn't afford to back down once the position he had been upholding (the agreed position of the shadow cabinet to seek amendments to Rudd's legislation) came under attack. If he tried to crash through, though, he would crash. To appease the rebels, shadow cabinet discussed a motion to defer the legislation if a deal wasn't reached. Even the Nationals were prepared to back negotiations, but the detail of the amendments provoked four hours of discussion. Andrew Robb spoke in favour. Nick Minchin made it clear that even agreement on all the amendments didn't guarantee party-room support for the final bill, and there was a group of Liberal senators prepared to cross the floor even if Turnbull won in the party room.

Turnbull's office was trying to assess what would happen in the party room if a deal was made. Nick Minchin's appearance on a *Four Corners* program investigating the Coalition's divisions on climate change provided some answers. Minchin's thoughts about climate-change being a plaything of the post-communist left were replayed across radio and television for days. He argued that climate change scepticism was the majority view in the party room. Minchin only ever spoke publicly with a purpose. If Turnbull didn't want to lead a party sceptical of climate change, that was fine with Minchin. Minchin's elected position as Senate leader was considerably more secure than Turnbull's hold on the party leadership.

Whenever Howard had sensed a strong minority viewpoint against him, he would avoid forcing a decision and retreat for consultation and compromise. If he needed to announce a decision, making his position clear to the party room was usually enough for a victory. In opposition, though, the leader has little control over the timing of parliamentary votes.

In an attempt to separate the issue from the leadership, some of the rebels made it clear that they expected Turnbull to stay on as leader even if the party room rolled him on the ETS. Yet the overlap between those lining up against an ETS and those complaining about Turnbull's leadership style was substantial. Claim and counter-claim about threats to pre-selection followed. A survey of the Liberal Party backbench appeared on the front page of *The Australian*, revealing that two-thirds of MPs did not support passage of the ETS ahead of what transpired at Copenhagen.[3] Only a handful of MPs and senators did not participate in the anonymous survey. It was the evidence loud opponents needed to prove they were not a minority. Deputy leader Julie Bishop quickly did her own ring-around to the backbench, reporting back to Turnbull that the survey was accurate and he therefore had a problem.

If hanging onto his job was Turnbull's primary motivation, he could have sabotaged the negotiations with the government. He made it clear, though, that he was not changing his stance. Bowing to what he considered a minority viewpoint would only invite further rebellions in future. Kevin Andrews ruling out a bid for the leadership would not normally make many waves. For a couple of weeks, though, colleagues had been encouraging Andrews to be the one who took a stand against Turnbull. Abbott was among those doing the urging, as part of his no-sniping policy. Andrews' ultimate role in bringing Turnbull down was why he was rewarded with a return to the frontbench in a senior position under Abbott's leadership. Andrews wanted Turnbull to know that the ETS was about the leadership after all.

The final deal included concessions in every area that Turnbull had asked for, but the level of compensation for polluting industries was a compromise. By any measure, Turnbull had extracted a good deal from the government. By any measure, that is, other than the purely political. Rudd made it clear that the same deal may not be on offer if a vote was delayed until 2010. Having said it was a good result, though, on what grounds could the prime minister justify producing a substantially different piece of legislation in a couple of months' time? The shadow cabinet would consider its position at 8 a.m. Tuesday, with the Coalition party-room meeting at 10 a.m. Those genuinely undecided had good cause to feel they were being railroaded by both Rudd and Turnbull. The shadow cabinet backed Turnbull. Only six out of twenty spoke against Turnbull's recommendation.

The length of the party-room debate was the first sign of trouble for Turnbull. For seven hours, Turnbull compiled two lists of names. With all backbenchers speaking, the numbers would be clear. Even a narrow win would leave him with little authority. 'I am not a barrister any more. I am not going to go out there and make a case for something I don't believe in,' he said at one point, eschewing one of the few great skills of political leadership he had brought to parliament from his previous careers. The tenor of the meeting was predictable until Andrew Robb rose to speak, arguing that the industry compensation was a long way from what the party room had originally sought. 'It's not good enough,' he concluded, prompting a fluttering of thumbs on mobile phones as the news was sent to waiting journalists. Robb received a standing ovation. His speech hurt Turnbull more than Abbott's defection, partly because Turnbull hadn't seen it coming and partly because Robb had acted for him against Nelson the previous year. At one point, after telling climate sceptic Alan Ferguson to 'get stuffed', Turnbull walked out. Nobody knew whether he was coming back.

Backbenchers were 41–32 against the deal. Turnbull added up shadow cabinet the way they had voted earlier in the day. Even including the Nationals, Turnbull reckoned he won 47–46. Opponents sent the room into uproar. The rules didn't matter; party-room discussions are about finding consensus and none existed on the ETS. At a news conference later, Turnbull's words couldn't have sounded emptier. 'I am the leader,' he said numerous times. 'I have made the call ... If people are unhappy with the leader they can take whatever steps they deem to be appropriate.'

Tuckey had already declared his intention to call a spill. Andrews was happy to be the stalking horse. Turnbull decided to call a meeting for the following day but didn't announce that until the next morning. Minchin and Abetz sounded out Hockey, who wasn't keen to meet the same fate as Nelson and Turnbull. Andrews went through the motions of declaring to the media what an opposition led by him would stand for. With Andrews the only declared candidate, 48–35 wasn't a convincing win in the secret ballot for the spill motion. While it was clear that Andrews was a proxy for anyone who wanted to oppose the leader, back in his office Turnbull couldn't believe that the pedestrian Victorian could attract a decent vote against him. He still wasn't getting his tone right. 'I am sure even somebody as quiet and unassuming as myself can improve,' he told Sky News shortly after the spill motion. 'We have all got to work on our interpersonal skills.' It wasn't clear which part of that was meant to be ironic. It was left to Hockey to assure everyone that Turnbull had been 'humbled' by the events of the week. The similarities to Abbott's February 2015 spill are remarkable.

Resignations from the shadow ministry began. Brett Mason, Mathias Cormann and Mitch Fifield freed themselves to vote against the bill. With talkback radio broadcasting the telephone numbers of Liberal Party offices, MPs had no shortage of advice from constituents. Turnbull was now paying for a feisty debate with 2GB host Alan Jones over climate change weeks earlier. Abbott and Minchin went to Turnbull's office to work out a compromise, knowing full well that it was an empty gesture. When Turnbull refused, Abbott, Minchin and Abetz quit the frontbench. Sophie Mirabella, Tony Smith and Michael Johnson followed, along with Senate whip Stephen Parry. Senator Fierravanti-Wells joined them the next day, citing the flood of complaints from voters as the most she had ever seen.

Though he maintained that his first preference was for Turnbull to stay on as leader, Abbott was rehearsing lines for the next election, likening the ETS to a new tax. It was only now becoming clear to Turnbull's colleagues that the ETS legislation, rather than the fate of the Coalition, was Turnbull's main concern. Scott Morrison reported that Turnbull was losing support among backbenchers. He was about to see the consequences of a lack of supporters prepared to fight to the end for him, but there was no way Turnbull was going to give his opponents the satisfaction of stepping down.

As unofficial leader of the moderates, Hockey held the key. If he continued to support Turnbull, it was possible the leader would prevail against Abbott. Abbott bared his torso for the cameras at Queenscliff Surf Club, if not looking like a Spartan warrior at least looking fit and healthy. Turnbull continued to lecture his colleagues through the media. 'If we put the party back together in accordance with Nick Minchin's wishes, then we will end up becoming a fringe party of the far right. John Howard's broad church is being shattered by Nick Minchin,' he told Laurie Oakes.

According to Hockey, Turnbull said if he lost the spill he would pull out. He didn't. The spill motion was carried 48–34. Many MPs were surprised to be voting in a three-way contest, not least Hockey. The moderates weren't prepared and some were sentimental enough to vote for Turnbull only to ensure he wasn't humiliated. Hockey trailed the field 23–26–35 to Turnbull and Abbott. The anyone-but-Abbott faction had a clear majority, but not if Turnbull was its candidate. Abbott prevailed 42–41. Remarkably, there was an abstention. Under the circumstances Turnbull had come amazingly close to hanging on.

There was only one consistent trend in public polling throughout 2009—the fall in Turnbull's satisfaction rating. Seizing the leadership from Nelson in such a ruthless way had rebounded on Turnbull. When the aggressor Abbott beat him by one vote, it almost ended Turnbull's political career. He announced plans to retire, only to be convinced by Howard not to depart if he wasn't truly ready. There is no way back from outside the parliament, Howard told Turnbull: 'Be sure of what you are doing.' Turnbull decided to stay, and Abbott returned him to the frontbench after the 2010 election. It eventually gave Turnbull a chance to rehabilitate himself with colleagues from the advantageous position of cabinet minister.

Not Enough Fibre

Turnbull maintained a relatively low profile while Abbott was prime minister in 2013–15. As Minister for Communications, he worked on vital areas such as media ownership and broadband, and as part of cabinet he did not necessarily have to comment on other portfolio areas. Turnbull's suspicion of the extent of government involvement in the technology sector he knew so well had begun in opposition. In 2009 Rudd and communications minister Stephen Conroy provided a tempting target for Turnbull to attack by unveiling another massive infrastructure program. Labor had promised a $4.7 billion broadband program during the election campaign but had trouble getting the tender process right once in government. Somehow, that plan morphed into an attention-grabbing $43 billion National Broadband Network. It was the sort of slipshod policy-making for which oppositions would be crucified but governments get away with by the sheer scale of the announcement. Multi-billion-dollar funding holes seemed like petty details. Tied up in the broadband plan was another provision to undermine the Howard government legacy—a threat to break up Telstra if it couldn't come to an agreement over sharing its network. Having made over $60 million from his founding stake in OzEmail, Turnbull knows something about the internet. He dismissed Labor's figures as 'la la land', and received some support from industry observers who couldn't make the numbers add up. Again, though, he couldn't unite the Coalition behind him, with a few Nationals reluctant to criticise regional infrastructure spending on such a scale. That division was less costly than some other episodes because the audacity of Labor's plan reduced Turnbull's criticism to what Peter Hartcher referred to as 'the last angry paragraph', the place in newspaper stories very familiar to opposition leaders.

Abbott ran a negative campaign against the cost of the NBN in 2010. By 2013 delays, cost blowouts and byzantine manoeuvring among incumbent telecommunications companies reduced the political advantages in Labor promising fibre to the homes of most Australians. However, the politics had now shifted from whether there should be an NBN to how it would work, and Turnbull was the responsible shadow minister. The bower bird preferred to pick and choose technologies as appropriate and as they emerged—something that would be more difficult in Labor's statist model. Under pressure to reduce the overall cost, though, Turnbull's alternative relied heavily on fibre to the node, with pre-existing copper—far from the latest technology—covering the remaining distance to the premises.

After two years of Turnbull as minister, there was little to show in terms of reduced cost or faster build. Telstra remained implacable. The inability to correctly forecast costs was not corrected. Overall costs were only fractionally improved over Labor's model when upgrading century-old copper was taken into account. The difficulties caused by such a large organisation changing strategy had been underestimated. Worst of all, the entire point of compromising on fibre to the house—a faster build—had been overrated. The Turnbull fix would be finished only a year sooner. The idea that Abbott had instructed Turnbull to sabotage the NBN is fanciful. Turnbull instinctively disliked the Labor approach but was unable to better it.[4]

Which Malcolm Would Become Prime Minister?

By early 2015, the growing likelihood of Turnbull as prime minister raised tantalising possibilities for insiders, commentators and political scientists alike. Abbott's biggest problem was the 2014 budget, which broke promises and seemed to exhaust the public's tolerance for endless economic reform that didn't ask for much sacrifice from the wealthiest Australians. There had been no sign, though, that Turnbull objected to any of these measures. Would he try to recast the Liberals as a more moderate political force? Could Turnbull improve the government's working relationship with the Greens, thereby helping the Coalition achieve greater policy outcomes in the Senate? The change of leadership within the Greens parliamentary party opened the door to a decoupling of the traditional Greens–Labor alliance, if the Liberals could find a way to take advantage of the change. Would Liberals and Greens consider preference agreements if common policy grounds could be found? And if Turnbull narrowed differences with Labor on some policy scripts, even occasionally outflanking Labor on the 'left', how would the opposition react?

The extent of the deal-making required to win the leadership vote is difficult to estimate. Thirty-nine Liberal MPs and senators had voted for an empty chair ahead of Abbott in a spill motion without a challenger, but as Cory Bernardi told us, there is every chance that number would have gone down not up had Turnbull nominated himself. Hardly a tribute to what so many MPs had previously seen of Turnbull as leader. No deals with the party's right had been done at that time. As we saw in the previous chapter, the end of Howard's tenure ushered in a period of shifting alliances. The likes of Scott Ryan, Michaelia Cash and Mitch Fifield had not yet come across to Team Turnbull. They were willing to give Abbott one more chance. Too many marginal-seat holders were more fearful of what Turnbull might offer than the lack of traction Abbott was getting in the polls back then. Deals had to be done—Turnbull knew it as did his inner circle, led by Arthur Sinodinos. Back in February even a plotter come September such as Peter Hendy was advocating a switch to Julie Bishop instead of Turnbull. Hendy had witnessed Turnbull firsthand during his time as Brendan Nelson's chief of staff. It didn't fill him with confidence. The deals important to Turnbull's garnering the numbers to bring down Abbott were always going to clash with expectations in moderate circles. They were unlikely to allow 'Malcolm to Be Malcolm'.

Turnbull had six years to reflect on his weaknesses between losing the opposition leadership and claiming the prime ministership from Abbott. The public had six years to forget them.

Approval-rating highs after Turnbull returned created hopes for a successful prime ministership, but the trend soon turned the other way. Younger voters must wonder whether a successful prime minister is even possible. The last prime minister to secure re-election with a majority was John Howard in 2004. Turnbull achieved the same in 2016, but only just.

One of the biggest costs of removing a prime minister is the lost machinery that operated in conjunction with the ousted leader. While there was a view that Team Abbott could have been better managed, and was behind the times in preparing for a difficult re-election, the 2015 changeover left Turnbull with little advanced preparation. The outgoing team was in no mood to offer the workplace handover that's traditional when jobs change. The outgoing PM certainly wasn't. And it is doubtful Team Turnbull would have taken such offerings even if they were made. The toxic relationship between Turnbull and Abbott's chief of staff Peta Credlin meant that changes at the secretariat were also necessary, given that Credlin's husband, Brian Loughnane, was the federal director. And the government also lost its Senate leader Eric Abetz, treasurer Joe Hockey and a host of senior players across staffing ranks. Abbott's deputy chief of staff Andrew Hirst made his way into the federal secretariat, but only marginally ahead of the election being called, to operate as the communications director for the party organisation. But much corporate memory went out the door when Abbott did.

For all the challenges such changes created for Turnbull, the bad blood attached to the change of leaders was the frontline cost, certainly in so far as the media was concerned. Journalists lined up to get a piece of Abbott while he was still angry, and for a while he was on a one-way path to emulating Kevin Rudd, before pulling back on the advice of those who cared for him and the legacy he would leave.

It didn't take long for this animosity to present itself. When Turnbull spoke after the party-room showdown on 15 September 2015, Abbott refused to shake the new prime minister's hand, and gave a blistering response to Turnbull's public advocacy that afternoon for the top job when addressing the party room. Colleagues recall Abbott turned to Turnbull and answered his pronouncements on polls and economic management one by one. There was no wishing him well, no graciousness in defeat. A large part of Abbott's anger was inevitably driven by his surprise in being removed that day, after landing from Adelaide unaware that numbers had already been gathered against him. One member of Abbott's leadership group points out the surprise was a sign of how removed the outgoing PM had become from reality. Recalling that Abbott used to 'will himself' to believe there was no way Turnbull would ever return to the leadership, the senior cabinet minister pointed out to us that 'despite forty-five staff, two whips in the house and more than enough warnings, Tony was so removed from reality that he still got a shock on the day of the spill'. Abbott and Credlin would contact newspaper editors to complain about commentators who used their columns to highlight the fact that momentum was building for a challenge. They would also complain directly to media proprietors, who would pass on to the editors what they were told. Credlin admits that she dismissed these commentators as 'lightweights' who overstated the quality of their sources. In the end it was Team Abbott who was ignorant of what was building under their very noses. The shock added to the cost of changing leaders, even if Turnbull enjoyed a joyous honeymoon.

His support for progressive ideas prior to commencing his political career was always misleading. A carefully crafted pragmatic agenda was always more likely, along with a central role for the economy. The wilderness years Turnbull endured between leadership stints had taught him that to be a 'successful' Liberal leader he needed to avoid pressing issues that risked splitting the party.

While Turnbull's leadership was rightfully expected to be different to Abbott's, or indeed Howard's, transformational change was never likely. Voters who expected genuine progressive agendas from their political leaders were always going to be disappointed by Turnbull's prime ministership, not due to a failure of leadership but to the context of his rise to power. There was never any doubt about Turnbull's dynamism and intellect, even if his political skills remain in question today. He was no institutionalist, though, and the limitations on the new prime minister were to a large degree institutional.

That Abbott was able to make his 'captain's calls' as prime minister in only trivial areas such as national honours showed the limited room a PM has to manoeuvre around the party, parliament and public opinion. Abbott's captain's call from opposition on paid family leave was decimated by these limitations once in office. The life-size bust of Winston Churchill Abbott put in his prime-ministerial office, which now adorns his much smaller backbencher's suite, was a cruel daily reminder of how much leadership has changed since the middle of the twentieth century. A growing budget deficit, sluggish economic growth and plummeting mining investment provided little capacity for any policy innovation that Turnbull might have favoured with big dollar signs attached.

Turnbull's elevation to the prime ministership in September 2015 raised the prospect of an embrace of progressive politics within the Liberal Party, but it was more mirage than reality. In truth he had courted Howard once Abbott turned his back on the former prime minister's advice; he had done the deals he had to with the factions and one-time opponents. And the net result was a realism in Turnbull that as Liberal leader he wouldn't be able to move too far out in front of his party on more than a handful of issues. The Liberal Party remains a conservative entity, and the moderate wing of the party has accepted the free-market orthodoxy for the most part. Turnbull is an illustration of this shift. This increases the degree of difficulty Turnbull would have if he tried to shift the party's philosophy too much or too quickly. Abbott was the leader of a reactionary wing that didn't simply disappear because he was deposed.

While Turnbull might display all the characteristics of an inner-city liberal, consider the team around him. George Brandis and Christopher Pyne share some of his beliefs, but the Manager of Government Business and the new Senate leader within Turnbull's government have been conditioned to pragmatic politicking for years in order to prosper under the revolving door of leaders since 2007. They survived the transition from Turnbull to Abbott in opposition, as well as the transition to government under Abbott's leadership, precisely because their views don't get in the way of a desire to stay at the apex of a conservative government. Just as Turnbull has been forced to shelve transformational leadership goals for largely transactional politicking, Pyne and Brandis are innately transactional, even if Brandis has an excellent historical understanding of liberalism and conservatism. Besides, they weren't really in the inner sanctum of the new Team Turnbull, with the exception of their formalised roles in the leadership team. Those who were—Sinodinos, Scott Morrison and, late in the piece, Julie Bishop—aren't all that liberal in outlook. Bishop has sidelined any such sentiments in order to become a darling of the West Australian Liberals, the most conservative division in the nation. She also over-compensates to avoid the tarring and feathering that sections of the right would like to bestow on her because of her decision to become a professional careerist woman. (How dare she.) Sinodinos was Howard's chief of staff—not the best CV builder for a moderate. And Morrison was the emerging leader of the right, including the hard right, before he did a deal with Turnbull to improve the party's chances of staying in power. The 'plotters', as they have come to be known, certainly aren't a bunch of moderates: Fifield, Ryan and Hendy all consider themselves right-wingers, just not right-wing fringe dwellers. Simon Birmingham, Wyatt Roy and James McGrath are moderates one and all, although McGrath would consider himself akin to Ryan in philosophical outlook. But it would be wrong to conclude that the forces that came together to install Turnbull were dominated by moderates.

The opinion polls had long shown that Turnbull was the preferred Liberal leader among Labor and non-aligned voters. His republicanism and support for marriage equality left many Australians hopeful that Turnbull would pursue those issues. That was always a vain hope. Turnbull took the leadership less than a year before an election. He needed first and foremost to re-establish the government's economic credentials without running into the problems caused by Abbott and Hockey's first budget. At the same time he needed to ensure that the execution of a first-term PM didn't see the party descend into political backstabbing. This required isolating the likes of Abbott, Eric Abetz and Kevin Andrews from the next generation of conservatives in the party. After the election Turnbull would do this by promoting next-generation conservatives, although naturally the conservatives don't think that he went far enough. Before the poll he did so with guarantees not to go back on the same-sex marriage plebiscite, not to 'radicalise' the government's climate-change agenda, and by targeting harder causes such as construction sector reforms to the building industry. But the perceived lack of promotions for next-generation conservatives in Turnbull's first ministry left them concerned that, if successful, Turnbull might seek to edge conservatism to the fringes.

Leadership theory has a long history in both political science and business. Modern politics has seen leaders in this country square off in a more presidential-style showdown. While individual electoral contests see the parties targeting seats where the margins are winnable, turning campaigning into a grassroots exercise, the national campaign is most influenced by the performances of the party leaders. Major party leaders have a tougher task than those running minor parties because they need to appeal to a broader cross-section of the community. And sometimes they need to appeal internally to the party in a different way to avoid challenges, or simply to win over members in the first place. This can damage a leader in the community if the party base is unreflective of the wider electorate.

Bill Shorten and Turnbull both faced internal problems as their head-to-head battle commenced. Labor's new leadership election rule—any spill requires a ballot of party members equally weighted alongside the caucus—gave Shorten security but he knew the man he defeated for the leadership in 2013, Anthony Albanese, would challenge him after an election loss if the margin was seen to be too great, despite the widespread consensus over the policy repositioning Shorten had led. His internal challenge, now and into the future, comes from the left. In addition to the Greens, Shorten had to pacify a growing power cohort who question his 'Liberal-lite' agenda. So far rank populism has been the antidote to this disease.

Turnbull's declining popularity in the electorate was complicated by internal battles, forcing him into policy positions he didn't necessarily believe in. Turnbull fell victim to both the political-science way of assessing leadership as well as the business motif of 'derailing'. Political leadership is most commonly assessed in a goal-oriented way. American presidential biographer and political scientist James MacGregor Burns wrote a seminal 1978 study on leadership, distinguishing between transformational and transactional leaders.[5] These types of leaders don't necessarily differ in their goals but in their means of achieving them. Transformational leaders seek to persuade the electorate of the need for change, pressuring political institutions by getting public opinion on their side. Transactional leaders achieve their goals through bargaining. The dichotomy neatly summarises Turnbull's predicament on assuming the prime ministership. As his attempt to persuade Australians of the need for a republic showed, Turnbull sees himself as a transformational figure. His own contrast with the arch-conservative Howard is instructive. While it has become de rigueur for conservatives to speak of reform, their goal is not transformation, but to make existing institutions efficient.

Modern politics is mostly transactional, meaning that a leader's hopes to be transformational are often dashed, damaging the leader's credibility in the process. Turnbull the transformational leader was quickly replaced by Turnbull the transactional prime minister. His personal polls crashed as a consequence. He began by establishing the need to remove Abbott on the basis of poor polls and poorer still economic leadership. Yet the new Turnbull government—riding high on the transformational hopes of small-l liberals—quickly retreated from major tax and federation reform, while simultaneously disappointing Abbott's ideological opponents by holding the conservative line on a multitude of policy issues. In Shorten, Turnbull would be facing the quintessential transactional leader, from his background in industrial negotiation to his record in counting heads in the Labor caucus.[6]

Turnbull is not a federalist. Malcolm Fraser was the last true federalist to lead the Liberal Party. Howard was a nationalist, with the government resources to provide national solutions in a host of areas. Abbott had floated a plan (vetoed by Howard) to take the running of hospitals away from state governments. As a prime minister with a growing budget deficit, though, Abbott saw the virtue in states taking on more responsibilities, reducing the rate of funding increases for schools and hospitals. Similarly, Turnbull would seek reform of taxation at the Council of Australian Governments to allow states to levy income tax. Abbott and Hockey had started work on tax and federation white papers but they weren't ready by the time of the leadership change, and Turnbull didn't like the policy direction, almost ensuring that genuine tax reform would not happen in the first term of government when parties have the most political capital to make such changes.

Fortunately for Turnbull, the Coalition has a longstanding advantage over the Labor Party when it comes to credibility on managing the economy, which helps explain why it sought to frame the election as a contest about 'who do you trust to run the economy'.[7] Labor couldn't afford to vacate this space lest it lose credibility, which was the purpose behind its ten-year forecasts for structural budget improvements championed by shadow treasurer Chris Bowen and his assistant shadow treasurer Andrew Leigh. But Labor also didn't want the showdown to be defined on this score. Shorten's campaign focused on health and education, with an added negative campaign depicting the government as being in the pockets of big business. The latter approach painted Shorten as a transformational leader—seeking to give political power back to average voters. To be sure, it was a negative form of envy politics, but it certainly wasn't seen that way by the growing number of voters who feel left out of the political system—those who pay little or no net tax yet demand that the big end of town pay more.

Turnbull was mindful of the need to change the way he did things as leader this time round. As prime minister without an election mandate, he owed too many favours to put his individual stamp on government. He would have to be more consultative on policy. Early leaks when ideas were being floated to a wide array of colleagues were a concern, but the decision was taken to continue consulting because the alternative—closing down lines of communications—was seen as a greater evil. Internal party research released to us after the election, however, showed that it was during the period of leaks on policy backdowns—throughout January and February 2016—that the most damage was done to Turnbull's brand in the wider electorate.

Notwithstanding a shortfall of funds during a long campaign, the move to Turnbull did help with party fundraising. Like leaders before him, Turnbull spent many nights during the campaign surrounded by donors dishing out the cash over private meals. And Coalition research showing enough marginal seats holding up to retain government was not what the research had revealed before the change of leader. It certainly wasn't the sense marginal-seat MPs had on the ground in their electorates, panic around which contributed to Abbott's demise. To escape from the transactional politics and institutional blockages Turnbull needed a mandate. But how and for what?

Three
AN AGILE START

IT WAS AN exciting time to be Malcolm Turnbull. He had restored the government's ascendancy in parliament and the electorate. Turnbull's Newspoll satisfaction rating peaked in November 2015 at 60 per cent. This post-Abbott relief rally was not destined to last long. There would be no snap election—the new prime minister's first captain's call. Turnbull wanted to govern and he wanted to go full term, believing that the stability this would deliver might help overcome the tumult of changing leaders the country had endured for over five years. Not everyone agreed. Christopher Pyne was the most vocal advocate for an early election, initially suggesting one for the end of 2015, then when the time for such a move came and went, he was equally as vocal pushing for a February or March early poll. By calling an early election Turnbull would assert authority on a divided party room with a thumping win, taking advantage of his honeymoon period as a new leader. Pyne urged Turnbull to make such a move in cabinet, within the leadership group and privately when talking to the prime minister. But Abbott was still wounded and may have derailed the campaign, just as Kevin Rudd did for Julia Gillard in 2010. Abbott's early behaviour confirmed as much.

He had promised no sniping but did want to get the record straight about his record. He accused the new treasurer, Scott Morrison, of 'badly misleading' the public over his role in the coup. Turnbull needed to be sure that Abbott would not sabotage a campaign. An early election also risked looking opportunistic, turning Turnbull into just another politician rather than the change agent. Turnbull was hoping to be seen to be rising above the politics of recent years, pitching himself as uninterested in 'three-word slogans', something journalists would wryly note when the 'jobs and growth' mantra was rolled out in the election campaign. Turnbull chose his own counsel not that of his close supporters such as Pyne when it came to avoiding the temptation of rushing to the polls.

Labor tried to attack Turnbull's wealth in Question Time. This was a mistake. Australians don't begrudge self-made millionaires. Questions on Turnbull's use of tax shelters may have been more fruitful for the opposition but were overshadowed by perceptions of the politics of envy. Portraying Turnbull as out of touch proved more successful for Labor during the campaign, when his background was linked to specific policy differences rather than class warfare. Labor frontbencher Tony Burke led the charge against Turnbull's wealth early on, and told colleagues not to panic that the negative messaging wasn't cutting through. 'It will,' he said, 'by the time we get to the election. This is just a foundation-laying exercise.'

The complex network of companies that Turnbull used to spread his fortune didn't exactly scream transparency. He also drew attention to his wealth by collecting the parliamentary travel allowance while staying in Canberra in a residence owned by his wife, Lucy—not the first politician to do so, but certainly the wealthiest. Turnbull had addressed questions about his wealth the first time he was leader. 'The Eastern Suburbs is a very eclectic area,' he said. 'It's very egalitarian notwithstanding there are areas of great prosperity. There are also areas of great social disadvantage. This electorate has the mansions of Bellevue Hill and the Matthew Talbot [refuge for the homeless] within, probably, 4½, 4 kilometres as the crow flies. I like the diversity of it.'

Some liberal commentators had totally unrealistic expectations once Turnbull reached the prime ministership. 'Already, after only a few weeks, the country feels different. The air itself has a new edge. And that edge has a name. Intelligence,' cooed *The Sydney Morning Herald*'s Elizabeth Farrelly. Such glowing tributes were deeply unhelpful, setting Turnbull up to fail. Of course, the constraints on policy reform caused by the way he came to power, as well as Turnbull's own prevarications and management of policy debates, didn't help.

Team Turnbull

The most important decisions in the short life of the Abbott government had come in the early weeks after the victorious 2013 campaign. Abbott had been advised that as useful as his chief of staff Peta Credlin had been in opposition, the chief of staff to a prime minister required a different set of skills. The strongest sign that Credlin was not playing the appropriate role was that she was constantly in the media—or, at least, her name and alleged activities were. In a sign that Turnbull was learning from Abbott's mistakes, the chief of staff he brought with him from the Department of Communications, Drew Clarke, is someone most Australians will not have heard of. More problematic for Turnbull was the political inexperience in his office. He needed a strong link to the organisational wing of the party and to his backbenchers.

Turnbull brought back strategists Mark Textor and Tony Nutt to the centre of the national team. Nutt, who had succeeded Arthur Sinodinos as Howard's chief of staff, had been party secretary in New South Wales. He had tried to return to federal duties under Abbott but couldn't get past Credlin. Party director Brian Loughnane was competent enough, but fresh thinking was needed when the government struck problems. The doubts, however, about Nutt soon built up. Was he really an agile new federal director? Most federal elections are tight contests, historically far more so than state showdowns. And with the likes of Mark Textor on the case the one thing Labor strategists feared was a cut-through advertising campaign driving voters to stick with the Coalition rather that 'risk' change. It never came.

It was never entirely clear why Team Abbott had kept Textor out of its inner circle. Labor's campaign organisation had long outperformed the Coalition's, especially considering the lopsided finances they frequently face. Abbott had frozen out one of the Coalition's best strategists. Many in the Liberal Party resent Textor's brash style and liberal social views—all of which have nothing to do with his ability as a pollster. It is likely this was as big an issue for Abbott, given his personality type, as it was for any other Liberal. Turnbull had no such reservations about Textor. Not only were their world views similar, but they had a relationship going back to when Textor did some private research for Turnbull in his electorate of Wentworth.

While Turnbull's supporters were rewarded in the new ministry, and many more women received a call-up to the cabinet, conservatives loyal to Abbott such as Christian Porter and Josh Frydenberg were also promoted to social services and resources respectively. Eric Abetz and Kevin Andrews were put out to pasture, a good decision on its merits but one that gave them time to make mischief. On balance, for the reasons we explained in the first chapter, Turnbull erred on the side of rewarding those who brought him to power. Only Craig Laundy from the core group of plotters missed out.

After the initial appointments and a reshuffle necessitated by the resignations of Mal Brough and Jamie Briggs, and the retirement of Nationals leader Warren Truss, there were six women in the cabinet. Kelly O'Dwyer as assistant treasurer and Michaelia Cash as Minister for Women joined Bishop and Sussan Ley. Fiona Nash was promoted when Truss retired. Replacing Andrews with NSW senator Marise Payne, a leading moderate whose career had stalled under Howard and Abbott, was the most eye-catching change. While this was laudable, these talented women were available for promotion only because they had won pre-selection to earlier parliaments.

Briggs had disgraced himself in a Hong Kong bar. Suggestions surfaced after the election that Foreign Minister Julie Bishop had orchestrated a review into Briggs's conduct that all but guaranteed he would need to resign. Briggs had been Joe Hockey's right-hand man when the former treasurer was campaigning behind the scenes for Bishop's then role as shadow treasurer during Turnbull's first stint as leader. It is not known if Turnbull was in on the take-down of Briggs, but he was certainly no Briggs fan. Briggs had only made it into the ministry when former small-business minister Bruce Billson rejected Turnbull's offer of an outer ministry position. Briggs was replaced by regional NSW MP Angus Taylor, one of the smartest of the young conservatives.

Brough also stood down during the summer break. His involvement in the Peter Slipper affair had caught up with him. Wyatt Roy was also on the margins of that investigation, but in the end the electorate got him first. Stuart Robert too was forced to resign from the frontbench over suggestions that he ignored a conflict of interest in helping a Liberal Party donor by attending a business meeting in an official capacity. The pressures and failures some of Turnbull's closest supporters faced emboldened criticisms among sections of the party's right, and it gave Labor the sniff it needed to re-establish confidence over a difficult summer.

The locus of power in Australian politics, though, is not entirely captured by the ministerial and staff appointments. Turnbull's kitchen cabinet varied issue by issue, usually in terms of strategic responses. If it was finance related, it was the Expenditure Review Committee (ERC), which included a mix of conservatives and newly promoted Turnbull supporters. Naturally Scott Morrison was there as treasurer. Finance minister Mathias Cormann stayed on the ERC from the Abbott era—the only permanent member throughout the lifetime of the Coalition in government. He was joined by Porter—who had been one of Abbott's parliamentary secretaries. Kelly O'Dwyer was on the ERC as the assistant treasurer, as was Sinodinos as cabinet secretary. In time Barnaby Joyce happily gained entry to the ERC courtesy of his elevation to the leadership of the Nationals. If it was a campaign tactic, discussions would initially be limited to Nutt, Textor and Sinodinos, with the wider leadership group brought in to confirm outcomes agreed to. Deputy Liberal leader Julie Bishop had a floating brief, given her close relationship with Turnbull, and the important role she had played in ensuring his successful elevation to the leadership. The leadership group was expanded from the definition John Howard had used to include managers of government business in both houses, all party leaders and deputies across both houses, as well as the treasurer, Morrison—a legacy from Joe Hockey's role in the leadership group of Abbott. As cabinet secretary, Sinodinos was added to this list. In total the number hit the dozen mark, and once the campaign started, leadership group hook-ups would start every morning before smaller strategic meetings were conducted. Even though Morrison was part of the leadership group, public questions emerged about whether he was truly included at the heart of government. Such doubts came about because of his absence on some of the smaller hook-ups, which, for example, agreed on the budget strategy without telling the treasurer before his regular morning-radio slot.

The dual tasks of maintaining harmony in the party room and hope among progressive voters who had felt shut out by the Liberal Party when Abbott was prime minister were near impossible. Expectation management was needed but there was little sign of it. By March 2016, Turnbull's disapproval rating had eclipsed his approval. The mistake made by many who had commented on Turnbull's initially high net satisfaction rating was not paying attention to the number of undecided respondents that distorted the results. As they almost inevitably moved into the dissatisfied column over time, the shine came off the new PM and the momentum moved in the wrong direction. Turnbull maintained his lead over Shorten as preferred prime minister but that only reflected the minimum level of competence of most incumbents.

Shifting Liberal Party policy away from Abbott's formulation would need to be a gradual process. Turnbull made his earliest difference where tone and rhetoric were important. Abbott would punctuate inclusive rhetoric on Islam with appeals to fellow conservatives. Turnbull was more consistent in arguing that Australia's security was best served by a Muslim community that was confident in cooperating with authorities. Every time the moderate Craig Laundy applauded the change in tone, the ultra-conservative Cory Bernardi felt further disengaged from his party leader. The irony being this pair get on well socially in Canberra during sitting weeks.

Turnbull's natural optimism provided another point of contrast to Abbott's style. While he overdid the bonhomie, and would eventually need to match rhetoric with policy action, there was plenty of reason to think that the government had given itself a second chance by dumping its most unpopular prime minister in history.

As well as continuing doubts about Turnbull's temperament and judgement, colleagues were frustrated with the way he came across in the media. For such a successful communicator in his previous occupations, Turnbull was surprisingly poor at the game of producing a good sound bite for the nightly television news. In combative interviews with *7.30*'s Leigh Sales or *Lateline*'s Tony Jones, he wanted primarily to win the debate instead of getting his message across. He was easily distracted by questions that most political leaders had long since learned to ignore. Ten years in parliament had hardly produced a single memorable performance in that arena. In longer-form interviews Turnbull was often debating himself, noting the flipside to his argument before the interviewer could raise the point. It was erudite but ineffective politicking.

Change with Continuity

With a snap election ruled out, Turnbull had time to assess the challenge in front of him. Delaying the election raised the expectation that Turnbull would put his stamp on policy. The bower bird collected shiny new gadgets. Turnbull had been one of the first Australian politicians with his own Facebook profile. He also got his hands on an Amazon Kindle reader before they were released in Australia. His official website featured a blog authored by his dogs (everyone's clever in the Turnbull household), though, sadly, the dog blog fell into disuse after Turnbull first won the leadership in 2008. He was an early adopter of Twitter. Keeping his pronouncements to 140 characters or less would be good discipline for Turnbull, who used his BlackBerry to respond to tweets. Kevin Rudd's feed was very dull and not very personal. Turnbull was well suited to the new medium but has become more conservative in using it as prime minister. As communications minister Turnbull had enjoyed posting pictures of himself using public transport as a contrast to Abbott's distrust of transport unions and the system they operate, documented in his book *Battlelines*.[1]

Innovation, then, would be an important portfolio. Turnbull appointed 25-year-old Wyatt Roy as Assistant Minister for Innovation, working under Christopher Pyne. Their science and innovation policy, launched a few months into Turnbull's prime ministership, promised $1.1 billion over four years. However, the background to this investment were the cuts under the Abbott government to universities and the CSIRO. Roy tweeted about his visits to every tech start-up in the country in the months after the policy launch. The policy's main features were greater certainty in science funding, changes to bankruptcy laws to encourage entrepreneurship, tax breaks for start-up companies, a tax offset for investors, funding for collaboration between industry and universities, computer-coding lessons for school children, and funding for 'landing pads' to give Australians a point of contact in tech-rich cities around the world such as San Francisco and Tel Aviv.

Landing pads for tech start-ups weren't much help to people not headed for Tel Aviv any time soon. Turnbull understood the danger of this sentiment, commenting that 'entrepreneurs create jobs, this is why we're doing so much to encourage new businesses'. Andrew Hastie, who was elected to the WA seat of Canning in a by-election shortly after Turnbull deposed Abbott, described a conversation with a constituent during the campaign. 'He couldn't understand the reason for company tax cuts, he wasn't earning enough to benefit from the increased tax thresholds and he wasn't an innovator—he was just an everyday Australian who was trying to pay down his mortgage and look after his children and ensure they had a brighter future,' he said, going on to take a shot at Mark Textor. Hastie, a social conservative, was no fan of Textor's brand of small-l liberalism, and felt that the campaign tactics that Textor helped oversee in the central office didn't work in outer metropolitan electorates such as his own. The fact Hastie had grown up on the other side of the country, in the plush eastern suburbs of Sydney, only moving into the electorate of Canning at the time Turnbull became leader during the by-election he was contesting, didn't prevent him offering forthright views on what did and didn't work in seats such as his. 'It had to be said,' he told a bemused senior colleague who had helped orchestrate Hastie's pre-selection for the seat. It was an early sign after the closely fought election result that the hard right within the Liberal Party wasn't going to make Turnbull's life easy.

Turnbull settled for continuity rather than change in most policy areas leading up to the campaign. Abbott's lethargy on tax and federation reform left a lot of tough policy work to do just months from an election, and here Turnbull would prove just as disappointing as his predecessor when it came to policy substance—but only after short bursts of bower bird–like nesting within various shiny policy objects. Sluggish revenue growth made tax reform both essential and difficult. Some of the issues where the differences between Turnbull and Abbott were sharpest were precisely those where the new prime minister had little room to move. Turnbull's position on gay rights, climate change and refugees placed him squarely in the left wing of his party. Either strong public opinion or a settled position within the government would prevent him from giving full effect to his personal beliefs. We had seen this from Turnbull in opposition in 2008–09 on the refugee issue, but not on climate change. As prime minister he therefore found it easier to emulate the rhetoric of Abbott on stopping the boats, albeit without the passion. The climate-change issue was more difficult, even if he had made his peace with holding differing views to his colleagues on the issue years ago. In interviews Turnbull would bat questions of inconsistency away rather than crawl back from his past commentary. Few on either side of the debate were satisfied by the responses. There was also continuity in the long-running debate over recognition of Aboriginal and Torres Strait Islanders in the Australian constitution. Abbott had run into conservative opposition to any wording that implied indigenous people have rights that do not apply to other Australians. The lack of consensus in indigenous communities had also delayed the long-promised referendum and those interested in this policy area despaired when the same-sex marriage plebiscite was so blithely placed on the agenda. To his credit, Abbott had showed, within his conservative world view, a great deal of interest in indigenous affairs, while it didn't seem a high priority for Turnbull.

While the same-sex marriage plebiscite may have started as a rear-guard conservative tactic to delay the inevitable, it solved a potentially intractable problem for the Coalition. Turnbull could preside over the change without reopening the divisive debate that had accelerated his predecessor's fall. The same-sex marriage debate in the Coalition party room had seen a majority in each party opposed to same-sex marriage, though the margin was greater within the Nationals. Liberal governments generally rely on their Coalition partner for a working majority, and even where they can govern in their own right the Coalition is rarely broken. While a Liberal leader isn't bound to limit their support for progressive policy settings within their own party because of the shared governing arrangements, the Nationals do have an impact on government policy. And close debates within the Liberal Party room are subject to informal influence by the Nationals.[2]

The public likes the idea of being asked policy questions instead of having parliament do its job. There shouldn't have been too many political problems associated with a plebiscite. A victorious government shouldn't have much trouble getting enabling legislation through the parliament; public assent would in turn ensure carriage of the relevant changes to the *Marriage Act*; and Bill Shorten would be exposed as a hypocrite when during the campaign footage emerged of him speaking in favour of a public vote in 2013, forcing him to clarify that he had since been persuaded that the debate surrounding a plebiscite would cause undue stress to gay and lesbian people. Despite all this, the government managed to look untidy on the same-sex marriage issue on numerous occasions. Brandis announced that the plebiscite would be held before the end of the year, only to be brushed back by the Prime Minister's Office. Having engineered the public vote as a way to delay what seemed like an inevitable change, conservatives in the Coalition reserved the right to vote against any legislation regardless of the public's verdict. Having fought hard to resist a conscience vote under Abbott, the likes of Eric Abetz and Cory Bernardi demanded one under Turnbull, after the multi-million-dollar plebiscite, irrespective of the result. It even emerged that some MPs wanted electorate-by-electorate breakdowns of the vote, so they could consider the will of their constituents before casting their votes in parliament. It became a farce. Enough ministers would have voted for change to make this issue irrelevant, but Turnbull was sensitive to unnecessarily riling the right of his party. He was happy enough with a conscience vote but cabinet had not confirmed the details of the plebiscite by the time the election was called, and the issue flared again in the last week of the campaign when Turnbull was trying to make his closing argument about stability in government. Senior figures within the campaign unit have told us not to underestimate the significance of this distraction, pointing out that conjoined with the Medicare scare campaign it sucked the oxygen out of the government's final week.

Turnbull had also made his peace with the Liberal Party on climate-change policy. Greg Hunt had long had a dual-track approach to this area of his portfolio. While Abbott was PM, he had ostentatiously played a role in replacing a market-friendly approach with Abbott's preferred interventionist approach, which Turnbull had previously labelled as an easy one to dismantle if the deniers prevailed in the climate-change debate. Hunt, meanwhile, designed the Direct Action system with safeguards that would allow a more market-friendly system of penalties and auctions in order to meet targets for carbon reduction. Indeed, while a carbon price is ultimately more efficient, any serious carbon-reduction strategy depends on a political consensus over emissions reduction that will cause pain to some consumers and businesses. No Australian government has proven willing to inflict that pain. Having learned something from his first experience of political leadership, Turnbull would not seek to re-embrace an emissions trading scheme; where Turnbull had once mocked Direct Action, he now presided over its rollout, with suggestions that he may widen the funding envelope for the scheme. His position on climate change back in 2009 had never been one of pure ideology. Turnbull had argued for a carbon price, believing that if the conservatives didn't do this they would suffer severe electoral repercussions at the hands of Kevin Rudd, given his advocacy for action to address the 'greatest moral and economic challenge of our generation'. Slowness to act on climate change had been a factor that harmed Howard in his quest to win a fifth straight election. The pragmatic origins of Turnbull's support for a progressive climate-change approach are crucial to understanding why he is now likely to be more pragmatic than progressively ideological. Indeed, Direct Action allows the bower bird to collect shiny objects such as solar panels and wind farms. Turnbull is fascinated by technology and leaving carbon abatement to the market takes the fun out of governing.

Refugee policy was in a different category. Like many small-l liberals in his party, Turnbull was eventually convinced by the deaths at sea on Labor's watch that a return to offshore detention was justifiable. Turnbull's rhetoric on boats as opposition leader in 2008 had been tough. As the refugee boats kept coming, Turnbull alleged that Rudd had 'put out the welcome mat' and 'lost control of Australia's borders'. While he was under pressure over the ETS debate in 2009, Turnbull deflected attention by criticising Rudd's approach to asylum-seekers, pointing out that unauthorised boat arrivals had increased more than ten-fold since changes to the law in 2008. Shadow immigration minister Sharman Stone had been saying as much for weeks without gaining much traction. Turnbull brought the issue to the centre of political debate, claiming that arrivals were 'going through the roof'. Responding to criticism from Malcolm Fraser and John Hewson, as well as the Labor government, that he was exploiting the issue, Turnbull channelled John Howard. 'It should not ever be controversial to state as a matter of policy and principle that Australians have the right to decide who comes to this country—our country—and the manner in which they come,' he said. That in 2015 Turnbull was not remotely interested in unwinding the measures put in place by immigration ministers Scott Morrison and Peter Dutton should have surprised nobody.

Turnbull was able to make little progress in another favourite policy area. Few policies are more suited to Turnbull than urban development. A bower bird can collect all manner of shiny objects in this portfolio area. A keen patron of public transport and an inveterate planner in spite of his free-market rhetoric, Turnbull liked the idea of bringing together innovative thinking in city planning and finance to improve quality of life and contribute to solutions to environmental problems.

With little money in the budget for his cities plan, Turnbull mused about leveraging state and private-sector investment. It was surprising, then, that little emerged in this area during the campaign. The one announcement Turnbull did make was jarring. He backed Labor's pledge to splash $100 million on a new football stadium in Townsville, the centre of Coalition MP Ewen Jones' seat of Herbert. Having criticised Shorten's announcement as confirmation of Labor's big-spending ways, Turnbull dressed up his similar announcement as part of his cities plan. However, that didn't overcome doubts about how little the stadium might actually be used and how little return taxpayers would see on their 'investment'. It contradicted his core campaign message and was so hastily put together that having a ministry for cities seemed pointless. That said, for a non-political prime minister it was an astute political move, and the closeness of the vote in Herbert vindicated the politics of the decision, even if it was poor public policy. In the end Jones lost the seat on a recount by 37 votes, leaving the state Liberal National Party to ponder a court challenge. Perhaps simply matching Labor's spending commitment without nuance would have secured the necessary extra votes. Turnbull was finding his transformational vision constrained by transactional politics in every policy area.

Cutting Tax Reform

Tax policy seems destined never to arrive for Malcolm Turnbull. As opposition leader in 2008–09, much work on this difficult area was done but not presented to colleagues before he was voted out. It became part of the mythology that a returned Turnbull leadership would see a new national tax reform plan. Part of this myth was that Arthur Sinodinos had a shadow budget prepared in 2015, in the event that Abbott's leadership fell over. It emerged, though, that Turnbull's new style was not to lead at all in this most complex and politically difficult of areas. He consulted about the need to reform but rarely offered his own position. He consulted experts inside and outside the public service. He consulted his colleagues. He consulted premiers, since long-lasting reform would have to tackle taxation at all levels of government. His apparent open-mindedness contributed to his initial popularity. Any concrete decision would undoubtedly reduce that popularity, but that was inevitable. He told Leigh Sales on *7.30* days after his election:

> The important thing is to be open-minded, consult, engage intelligently, explain the challenges to the public in a manner that respects their intelligence and then make a decision, and having made a decision, then argue, advocate, in other words, why your decision is right.

Turnbull's open-mindedness on lifting the Goods and Services Tax left Labor a point of attack. Labor was on safe ground in opposing a rise in the GST even when one was not being proposed. That position united the party and bound them to the public in a warm-up for Mediscare during the campaign.

Many inside the government were ready to wear the political risk of a GST increase if a reform package could be constructed. The problem was crafting adequate compensation. For the same reason that the GST is an efficient tax favoured by economists and big business, it hits consumers hard. When the GST was introduced, it replaced other taxes but also raised some new revenue, providing sufficient funds to over-compensate interest groups and make the political costs manageable. A greater proportion of GST revenue from any subsequent increase would be required for compensation. With the expectation that income tax cuts would be part of the package, Treasury simply couldn't make the sums add up. This, however, was both logical and predictable. Treasury could have presented Turnbull with this kind of analysis on his first day as prime minister. Instead, he had raised expectations of reform, encouraged colleagues to take political risks and given Labor a stick with which to beat the government. And he had wasted six precious months in doing so.

The GST never even seriously got to cabinet. It was knocked on the head during the Expenditure Review Committee process, but only after the treasurer had briefed journalists on the need to enact such a change 'as an inevitability', before a walk-back became the option Turnbull preferred. The GST debate put the PM and the treasurer on a collision path. They took over their respective positions with quite different views on the subject. Turnbull was open-minded, but felt genuinely persuaded against action by the evidence. Scott Morrison had Peter Costello in his ear, regaling him with stories about what he had done as treasurer during the Howard years, leaving Morrison with the impression a bold move on the GST was his ticket to accolades (in time), making him a worthy promotion to the treasury portfolio. Morrison presumably also saw such robust policy-making as a credibility driver beyond his success in stopping the boats, turning him into a multi-layered alternative PM in the years to come. Turnbull was more interested in bedding down his prime ministership with a majority of his own at an election, and hence he worried about selling GST changes. Turnbull, perhaps rightly, believed that the complexity of doing something now on the GST was far greater than in Howard's day, partly because politics had become more difficult, partly because of the institutional impediments the deal Howard struck had put in place. The meandering path to this decision had given time for Labor's campaign against a GST rise to bite in marginal seats. Backbenchers returning in 2016 from the summer break gave voice to their concerns in the party room and in the media. For their part Labor saw Turnbull's capitulation on the GST as a sign of weakness. While they relished the opportunity to get a scare campaign on the GST changes right (copying Paul Keating in 1993, not Kim Beazley in 1998), they felt equally buoyed by the fact Turnbull had squibbed it and seemed to be on a different page to his treasurer.

Turnbull wasn't finished his game of raising and then dashing expectations of bold policy-making. Not by a long way. Australia is unusual around the world in allowing losses on investments to be deducted against other forms of income. It sounds egalitarian that salary earners can join capitalists in offsetting profits with losses until you realise that the vast bulk of the benefits go to high-income earners. The government was willing to confuse this issue by pointing out that the largest numbers of individuals negatively gearing property were not far above the median income. But the middle is the meaty part of any bell curve. The financial benefits accrue to those with a fourth, fifth or more properties, and not many of them were the police and nurses Treasurer Morrison loved to mention as those benefiting from negative gearing.

Turnbull had mused about limits on negative gearing, or limits on income tax deductions more generally, prior to Labor releasing its own policy. As in other areas, Bill Shorten was willing to lead. Unlike with superannuation, the government was not prepared to follow this time. Labor had long foreshadowed restrictions on negative gearing, but to mount a scare campaign against its policy could be difficult, given the number of Coalition frontbenchers who had expressed concerns about the 'excesses' in current negative-gearing laws. The issue was debated in cabinet, with Peter Dutton, Josh Frydenberg and Christian Porter arguing against making any changes. Only Porter within that trio was also a member of the ERC. Dutton pointed out the political value in doing nothing so as to attack Labor's changes 'with clean hands'. When the debate was had within cabinet the PM, treasurer and assistant treasurer Kelly O'Dwyer were all in favour of making changes, but doing so in a 'more considered' and 'less extreme way' than Labor had. Cabinet didn't ultimately take a position one way or the other, and the ERC ended up knocking the idea of changes on the head before any formal proposal went from the finance team to cabinet. We were told that Mathias Cormann, as finance minister, joined Porter within the ERC to challenge the value in making changes, convincing the PM and Morrison to back down. As the most junior member of the ERC, O'Dwyer went along with the broader view. Turnbull would later argue that Labor's limits on negative gearing, combined with reducing the capital-gains tax discount, formed 'a big sledgehammer they're taking to the property market'. Asked by Leigh Sales about the evidence for his claims, Turnbull fell back on 'common sense' and 'the laws of supply and demand'.

Abbott had been more reactionary than conservative on many policy fronts during his prime ministership. National security was a common policy area where reactive policy-making took precedence over a traditionally cautious conservative approach to hastily announced and drafted laws designed to address emerging challenges. Turnbull sought to alter some of Abbott's reactionary positioning around social and cultural issues, little changing other than the rhetoric in the national security space, but only once he had entrenched his own position and established dominance over Labor in the area of economic policy. Generational renewal would assist to alter these views, with the likes of Abbott and Kevin Andrews being replaced by temperamental rather than ideological conservatives. The social-services portfolio was handed to a rising star among conservatives, West Australian Christian Porter, who worked diligently in a demanding portfolio without the ideological warfare that Andrews had brought to the role. The budget confirmed a less hard-line approach to welfare. It also raised uncertainty about the future of a favourite Howard and Abbott policy, with funding for the school chaplains program not provided in the full four-year forward estimates.

The Council of Australian Governments meeting in late March 2016 saw Turnbull encapsulate the flaws of his prime ministership in forty-eight hours: passionate advocacy followed by a backflip and moving straight onto the next shiny object. Turnbull's proposal for states to levy a portion of income tax was doomed when journalists dubbed it 'radical'. It was hardly that, having been floated by any number of prime ministers and premiers since income tax powers were granted to the Commonwealth during World War II. Turnbull didn't help this perception, dubbing the plan that the assembled premiers had not been consulted about 'the most fundamental reform to the federation in generations'. NSW premier Mike Baird, having shown leadership in the GST debate, was non-committal, but the Labor premiers, led by Victoria's Daniel Andrews, were having none of it—dismissing Turnbull's 'thought bubble'. Federal shadow treasurer Chris Bowen leaped on the notion of 'double taxation'. With little detail to back his position, Turnbull withdrew the proposal. Baird had apparently offered some support for the idea over the phone, but that was never on display once the idea went public. All of this activity may have been more understandable as part of a longer-term strategy to justify subsequent tough measures, having established that the states were unwilling to pay for services and infrastructure. None were likely, though, so close to an election. More tellingly, such political strategising appears beyond Turnbull's political capabilities.

Turnbull had to move to the right in policy areas he would not naturally feel comfortable doing so in order to appease discontent among conservatives. While many of them might not have lamented the loss of Abbott as a leader (he let down his conservative base every bit as much as he did the rest of Australia), conservatives would fight hard to prevent the Liberal Party shifting its ideological positioning under Turnbull. Hard-right fringe conservatives would fight even harder, and their impact was magnified by a distorted media representation of conservatism, which is arguably more reactionary in style. Ageing white male newspaper columnists and broadcasters were the largest part of the delcon phenomenon, and they came out in force to shout down Turnbull.

Labor's Woes

Given the eventual result, it is interesting that Shorten was under more pressure than was publicly understood at the beginning of the election year. In January 2016 there was a genuine push to replace the Labor leader, instigated by the left, with Mark Butler making the calls on behalf of Anthony Albanese. Butler is a senior figure in the left of the Labor Party, and a prominent frontbencher hailing from South Australia. He has long been seen within Labor circles as one of Albanese's closest supporters. Having been elected Labor Party president he is also seen as a future contender for the parliamentary leadership of the party, although Butler himself has said that he has no such ambitions. It is hard to establish what exactly happened—whether they were mere soundings, a genuine effort to bypass the new leadership rules to oust Shorten, or simply the laying of foundations for a post-election strike if Shorten's campaign was underwhelming. Since the election, Shorten has been confirmed in the leadership for the next three years, barring some sort of orchestrated early removal. But even that was far from certain in the days immediately after the election, and it is evident that at the start of 2016 Shorten was vulnerable to a tap on the shoulder, as one-time friends and enemies found agreement: Turnbull's ascension to the prime ministership had weakened Labor's chances at the looming election. Supporters of Albanese were searching for allies to oust the unpopular opposition leader. While Shorten's preferred PM numbers matched Abbott's, once the Liberals changed leaders Shorten's standing plummeted. It stayed there through the summer months and even Senate leader Penny Wong began expressing her dismay to colleagues about the differential.

Albanese supporters targeted the NSW right, which had always had doubts about Shorten despite being of the same faction. The Victorian right is a brotherhood; for them the bonds are personal. They would never desert their local man Shorten. This meant that the likes of Stephen Conroy, David Feeney and Mark Dreyfus were rusted-on Shorten supporters. It was different for the NSW right, which has a more transactional view of loyalty. Whatever the intended nature of the approach from Albanese supporters, the NSW right took it as a sign the left was prepared to move on Shorten. The NSW right members were amenable. The bait was the offer of the deputy's position to the shadow treasurer Chris Bowen. It left some wondering how Tanya Plibersek might feel about that. She didn't control numbers as such, but she was popular with the public, and dumping a female deputy who had done nothing wrong for the purpose of purely factional deal-making wouldn't be the best look.

While Butler came from one of the smaller states, when the right-wing smaller state members were approached to see if they would join forces with a cross-factional grouping that included much of the left and the NSW right, most demurred. The plan collapsed when Shorten embraced Bowen's idea of negative-gearing reform on 14 February. It contrasted with the capitulation of Team Turnbull on tax reform followed by federation reform. Shorten stood for something, which won him points even from the highly transactional NSW right. Bowen was impressed, and withdrew his tacit support for the manoeuvring that was going on. Tony Burke continued to agitate but many of his factional colleagues assumed that he simply wanted the baton to pass on more quickly to ensure his own progress up the pecking order. Later in the campaign Shorten would lose the confidence of much of the NSW right when he refused to tighten his fiscal belt at the expense of spending on health and education. Bowen and others lost internal battle after internal battle on such matters, and only the sheer quantum of seats Shorten picked up saved him from a post-election leadership challenge, and a fracturing of the national right.

This was just how close the NSW right came to supporting a post-election leadership challenge from Albanese, notwithstanding the performance of Labor at the election. The NSW general secretary, Kaila Murnain, had to 'talk them off a cliff', as one unconvinced member of the right put it to us. Again, Burke was agitating for a challenge, which helps explain why after the election Shorten shifted him out of shadow finance and into a part-time environment portfolio that doesn't even include climate change. It carried the added bonus for Shorten of stripping portfolio responsibilities from Albo's spear-carrier Butler, who was left only with climate change. Shorten also neatly outmanoeuvred his internal critics, bringing forward the timing of the caucus meeting and asking Albanese to move the motion supporting Shorten's retention of the leadership. Albanese was understandably upset when Shorten leaked this fact to the media before Albanese had the chance to say so himself. It was unnecessary because Albanese had already given his word that he would do it. Shorten was ringing journalists, bragging that he had been underestimated during the campaign, had outsmarted Albanese and the left, and he was positioned exactly where he needed to be for the parliamentary term. He was supremely confident.

The leadership tensions on the Labor side were a constant presence throughout the campaign and even immediately after Shorten's better than expected showing. But in the context of Turnbull's challenges leading up to the campaign, Shorten's tenuous hold on his leadership barely seeped into the public domain. Turnbull had no such luck—from the moment he ousted Abbott as prime minister, the delcons were after him.

Four
THE DELCONS

THE DELUSIONAL CONSERVATIVES (delcons) by their own admission spent the night of the election barracking for Malcolm Turnbull to fail. Text messages were flying between the unofficial grouping—some while on air covering the election for television and radio, others hosting small parties to toast what they hoped would be a repudiation of Turnbull, a man they had long loathed. In the days that followed the election some called for Turnbull to resign, claiming that the result was utter failure, demanding Tony Abbott be returned to the leadership. Andrew Bolt even appeared on Sky News's election-night coverage halfway through the count and demanded Turnbull resign. The premature landing by Bolt turned Alan Jones into the voice of reason. He appeared shortly after to refute the idea. Unhappy as Jones was with Turnbull's performance he told viewers that the last thing Australia needed was another PM in quick succession. He defended Turnbull's right to carry on, hoped Shorten wouldn't win and that Turnbull would lift his game. It was a lucid performance from one of Abbott's closest allies in the media, separating him from the delcon pack.

Conservative columnist Miranda Devine coined the term 'delcon', for 'delusional conservatives', and it was quickly picked up by Niki Savva, columnist for *The Australian*. Devine was thinking about her ideological fellow travellers, mostly in Sydney, who hoped that Labor would win the election to punish the Liberals for the change to Turnbull. She also found their collective advocacy for an Abbott return delusional. While Bolt must have assumed that the coined term was being directed at him, given some of his responses to it on his blog, that wasn't Devine's initial intention. She was thinking about the likes of head of the Menzies Research Centre Nick Cater, journalist Rebecca Weisser, that most polemic of academics James Allan from the University of Queensland, Paul Murray from Sky News, Rowan Dean from *Spectator Australia*, former head of Treasury John Stone and even Greg Sheridan, foreign editor at *The Australian* and long-time friend of Abbott. Tom Switzer from the US Studies Centre is another, as is John O'Sullivan from *Quadrant* and editorial writer at *The Daily Telegraph* Tim Blair. The delcon phenomenon is more prevalent within the commentariat than the parliament. That said, Kevin Andrews is certainly a member, as is Eric Abetz. While Devine probably wouldn't agree, we have labelled new MP Andrew Hastie an apprentice delcon. Cory Bernardi runs with the delcon pack, but he is more of an 'anyone but Turnbull' club member. Bernardi saw Abbott's faults as PM long before most others did.

Reality has never impinged on the delcons' delusions about Abbott, certainly not in the wake of a close election showdown. Many continue to spruik for his return, pointing out that Kevin Rudd managed a comeback that also appeared unlikely. The difference is that Rudd never trailed in thirty consecutive Newspolls like Abbott did. Cheeky polling comparing Labor led by Rudd versus Julia Gillard also stoked tensions after the 2010 result. It is unlikely Abbott would poll as well as Rudd did. Equally, a new generation of conservatives in parliament has expressed zero appetite for a return to Abbott. They didn't even support Abbott returning to the frontbench after the election, much less the leadership. Modern politics has taught us never to rule anything out, but an Abbott comeback would outrank all other unexpected turns of events in recent Australian politics. And yet he is doing the rounds.

Like many observers, the delcons drew premature conclusions on election night. The final result confirmed that Turnbull did secure a majority and Bill Shorten won only 69 seats, barely more than Kim Beazley had won at the 2001 election, a result that had been toasted by conservatives right around the country. And it was Labor's second-lowest primary vote in history. As we have seen, though, Turnbull's response on election night wasn't altogether rational either.

The delcons want to rewrite the history of the Abbott era in spite of their own criticism of him for walking away from many of the policies they were passionate about, such as changing section 18C of the *Racial Discrimination Act*—which conservatives and some liberals see as stifling freedom of speech.[1] And, of course, Abbott introduced the 'temporary' deficit levy that they railed against. They now lionise Abbott not because they were satisfied with his performance as prime minister, but because of their loathing for Turnbull—who, going back to his time running the Australian Republican Movement, has been a figure of disdain for many conservatives. The delcons were isolated by Abbott's chief of staff Peta Credlin before or soon after Abbott won the prime ministership. They henceforth became some of his biggest critics. Delcons thrive on attention, and Credlin distracted Abbott from the all-important task of paying attention to these commentators. It was a distraction built around her desire to control access to Abbott, but it had the effect of turning allies into critics. But after Abbott's 'near death experience' in the leadership spill of February 2015, Credlin made a point of extending the hand of friendship to those delcons whose criticisms of her had been relatively tame. By the time of Turnbull's challenge, the delcons were outraged anyone would dare remove a PM who had trailed in the polls for eighteen months and failed the test of consultation with parliamentary colleagues. Just as Turnbull had to compromise to find support, conservatives looked forward to more influence as Abbott sought to hang on to what he believed was rightfully his—something only voters could strip from him. Since being out of office Abbott has had even more time to devote to conversations, text messages, coffees and dinners with various delcons. The lines of communication help fuel their collective desire to bring Turnbull undone, even if Abbott isn't necessarily egging on such conduct.

There is little doubt that Turnbull's performance at the 2016 election fell short of expectations, but those same expectations were inflated beyond what was attainable in a volatile political climate. While he added to the difficulties of succeeding with some messy politicking, as well as poor policy development, the real questions for this chapter are who are the delcons and why do they hate Turnbull so much? With their having invested so much emotional energy in hating Turnbull, is there even a narrow pathway for Turnbull to bring them back into the fold, or will he face a permanent rump on his right flank that watches, waits and hopes for his downfall?

Who Are the Delcons?

Abbott was on his annual charity Pollie Pedal when the first Newspoll showing the government trailing under Turnbull's leadership was published in April 2016. Internal polling from January and February had already identified a drift away from the government and the new PM. Turnbull had used Newspoll as a yardstick for the Abbott government's intractable problems. One poor result under the new prime minister was a long way from the thirty consecutive polls that had prompted the move against Abbott, though. Many of those polls had showed the Coalition well out of striking distance from Labor, and Abbott had dismally low personal approval ratings and was behind Shorten as preferred prime minister for a sustained period of time—including the point at which Turnbull challenged him. Abbott had also broken any bond of trust he'd had with voters by going back on his promises in the 2014 budget. Central among the backflips were the cuts to health, making it simple to imagine how much more potent the Medicare scare campaign would have been against Abbott. This assumption was borne out by strategist Mark Textor's focus group research during the campaign.

While Abbott himself was circumspect about the latest Newspoll finding, some of his supporters couldn't hide their glee at their own party's mixed fortunes. Coinciding with news that Kevin Andrews had told his local paper he might once again offer his services as leader at some future point, it was all too much for *Daily Telegraph* columnist Miranda Devine, who dubbed the small band of Abbott diehards 'delcons'. Devine was one of a select number of conservative journalists invited to Kirribilli House in Sydney shortly after Abbott's election win. Her critique of Abbott as prime minister was that he was insufficiently conservative, failing the right on freedom of speech, the deficit levy on high-income earners and other deviations from policy purity. 'Abbott was no conservative prime minister,' she concluded. She was also a harsh critic of Credlin, which is why, unlike other conservative commentators, Credlin didn't court her after the February spill. Devine showed courage standing up to some of the stupidity of the delcons, given that many of them were her natural ideological allies, even friends.

Abbott's removal as prime minister wasn't a rebellion against his philosophical positioning—even if some of Abbott's decisions revealed a large gap between his beliefs and those of the electorate. Indeed, it is questionable whether Abbott really moved the party in most policy areas onto a more conservative footing than it had been under John Howard's leadership. Abbott was heavily criticised by his 'base' early on in his prime ministership for his generous paid maternity leave proposal and his retreat from a commitment to amend the *Racial Discrimination Act*, for example. In the end Abbott's base fell in behind him despite reservations about his leadership. This was partly a cultural response to threats to a first-term prime minister, and partly to block Turnbull.

While Devine didn't particularly want Turnbull to replace Abbott, she had no personal loyalty to the former prime minister and wrote many times about the dysfunction of his office. The greatest sin in Devine's eyes was that some Liberal Party supporters were touting their intention to vote for Labor as long as Turnbull remained leader. Law professor James Allan wrote that his initial position of an informal vote protesting the leadership change was not strong enough and he would be voting Labor. Former Treasury secretary John Stone advocated tactical voting, shunning Liberals who had voted to oust Abbott in favour of conservative independents or, where possible, the National Party (not a great surprise for a former National Party senator). 'If treachery and betrayal on this scale are not punished,' Stone wrote, 'they will beget more such treachery and betrayal, as Labor Party experience amply demonstrates.' Stone preferred the term 'dis-con'—disconnected conservative—rather than delcon. Strangely, this term failed to take off. No commentary was more delusional than Maurice Newman's comic turn railing against elites—as though a former chair of the stock exchange scrapes the dirt from under his nails each time he hits the keyboard to write yet another column in praise of Abbott. Newman called again for a return to Abbott in his first column after the election. 'The Delcon movement is tiny but viciously punitive to those it regards as heretics,' Devine wrote, sharing with her readers some of the viciousness that Twitter seems to reserve for women with a strong opinion. 'One long dummy spit,' was how *The Australian*'s Niki Savva described the delcons.

According to Devine, many conservatives were 'encouraged in their delusions by a lucrative new industry of talking heads, whose bread and butter is political turmoil'. A similar critique has emerged of notional Republicans in the United States whose primary allegiance is not to the Republican Party but to a 'conservative entertainment complex' that thrives on conflict instead of policy analysis and institution-building.[2] Surely *Spectator Australia* editor Rowan Dean was more performance artist than political commentator when he wrote during the campaign that were he still leader Abbott would have 'taken what little credibility remains of Labor and slammed them not only out of the ballpark but over the road'. Some delcons, like Devine's fellow *Daily Telegraph* columnist Tim Blair, underlined Devine's point by embracing the slight. Andrew Bolt wasn't so fond of the term, preferring to label Turnbull supporters as delusional, and taking a victory lap on election night. The high-handed criticism of the pointed use of the term 'delcons' was hard to swallow when these same commentators kept using the term 'bedwetters' to describe anyone who had dared to vote for Turnbull in the leadership spill. Abuse and name-calling had to be a one-way street to be acceptable. Broadcaster Alan Jones had a more complicated relationship with Turnbull, regretting the leadership change but mending his relationship with Turnbull prior to the campaign.

'Blue on blue violence' was how Labor's Nick Champion chose to cheerfully describe what was going on. Yet few MPs could be described as delcons. Led by cabinet ministers such as Cormann, Dutton, Porter and Frydenberg, conservative MPs saw their interest squarely as helping to achieve the best possible election result. With no future in politics without an Abbott return, Abetz and Andrews tried but failed to recruit younger MPs to the delcon ranks. It was this 'Dad's Army' of supporters, more so than Abbott himself, who planted stories during the campaign. Sometimes the politicians backgrounded their fellow delcons, who dutifully reflected their concerns. Sometimes the politicians raised concerns directly via media appearances. And of course most delcons had regular media platforms of their own to fill the airwaves and column inches with attacks on Turnbull. Publicly, Abbott gave every appearance of putting what he referred to as the 'disagreement' within the party in 2015 behind him, as though a year of trench warfare was just a polite misunderstanding. In the first week of the election campaign, Abbott cut a lonely figure handing out campaign material to uninterested commuters running through the rain to catch the Manly ferry. The best outcome for Abbott would be a poor Turnbull performance without the perception that Abbott was publicly undermining the government, particularly in light of his comments when he was deposed about not carping and sniping.

Considering the eight-week campaign left the media with ample time for distraction, there were few outbreaks of disunity in the parliamentary ranks of the government. Just over the halfway mark, journalist Phil Coorey wrote that Turnbull would be under pressure to appoint Abbott to cabinet 'in the event of a modest election win'. Turnbull reasonably pointed out that there would be no room for new cabinet positions in the event of a Coalition win, although it turned out a couple of spots in the ministry did open up due to lost seats. The story didn't seem to originate with Abbott—Coorey cited 'colleagues of the former prime minister'—suggesting that some in the party were more than happy to make mischief for their own party in the middle of a tight election campaign. Those colleagues showed the depth of their delusion when they nominated defence as a likely portfolio. Given Abbott's judgement as prime minister in seeking to deploy troops to anywhere from Ukraine to Kurdistan, having to be talked down by cooler heads, this never seemed likely.[3] The story died after Turnbull's statement but was revisited once the modesty of his victory was known. More grumbling came from the delcons when Turnbull told *Four Corners* that the government would have lost 'very resoundingly' if Abbott had still been prime minister.

Meanwhile, the high media profile of Abbott's former chief of staff Peta Credlin only reminded government insiders of the dysfunction in Abbott's office, the tales of bullying, as recorded by interviews ex-staffers did after Abbott was deposed, many of which were on the record.[4] The public got a sense of what the pressure must have been like in a tightly controlled Prime Minister's Office—with retribution and threats always present—when Peta Credlin used one of her many Sky News appearances to tell Andrew Bolt that people 'haven't seen nothing yet' by way of payback. She was in a position to keep her promise, having orchestrated much of the delcon commentary via text messages to her colleagues at Sky News now that she was on the books as a contributor. But realising the damage to her personally when seeing the statement replayed throughout the following morning on Sky News, she suggested that it be withdrawn from bulletins, which duly happened—one of many perks she enjoyed by joining the media fraternity.

A week before the election a Galaxy poll asked respondents about their vote were Abbott still prime minister. The Coalition primary and two-party-preferred votes crashed, as they had when he actually was leader. A 47–53 per cent two-party vote was in the offing—making the gamble on Turnbull a winner for most Liberal MPs nursing small margins. Among them was Luke Howarth, who held the most marginal Liberal seat anywhere in the country—Petrie. He retained it with a swing to him. Another marginal-seat holder, Craig Laundy, who had backed Turnbull in the September showdown in 2015, also increased his majority. He hadn't thought he could win under Abbott's leadership, and contemplated not even contesting the 2016 election if the push to remove Abbott failed. Conservatives such as Michael Sukkar in the electorate of Deakin can thank Turnbull for prolonging their parliamentary careers, for without the change of leadership, internal polling showed that Victoria was a bloodbath for the Liberals, with three if not four seats in Labor's sights.

Three days before the election, Abbott reflected on the campaign with Paul Murray on Sky News. He praised Turnbull's 'statesman-like' performance. The stoush with Turnbull was 'all dirty water under the bridge'. He couldn't help, though, but muse about how things might have been handled better. 'A lot of big issues have been touched on without really being developed,' the great developer of issues pronounced. 'Obviously there is a huge budget repair job that needs to be done … If those big issues aren't front and centre then less substantial stuff will be front and centre,' Abbott said, taking his cue from Murray's complaint that the undecided details of the Coalition's proposed plebiscite on same-sex marriage had dominated the previous couple of news cycles. 'National security has played almost no part in this campaign,' Abbott continued. The government had in fact manufactured some news on boat non-arrivals, but it's much harder to make news out of asylum-seekers without the visual component of the boats—a problem Abbott himself experienced after the initial success of his turn-back policy. He made a laughing stock of himself by continuing to remind Australia that he had stopped the boats long after the issue had slipped down the political agenda. What Abbott said off camera was apparently far more interesting and instructive as to his state of mind about the man who had replaced him in the top job. Television journalists covering politics often make this observation.

As for budget repair, it was two days before the 2013 election that Joe Hockey delivered the Coalition's response to the 'budget emergency' he and Abbott would inherit from Labor. After outlining the opposition's costings, Hockey asserted that he could balance the budget with 'no cuts to health, no cuts to education, no changes to pensions and no changes to the GST'—a line Abbott made immortal on election eve. The main reason why the public didn't trust the Coalition's promises on the budget was because Abbott had broken so many, and then had the front to deny doing so in all cases but one—ABC cuts. The delcons were just as mistaken about which policies were to blame for the Abbott government's unpopularity as they were about who was to blame for his downfall. There was a long history to their antipathy to Turnbull.

Party Man

Conservative antipathy towards Turnbull can be attributed to his beliefs and his personality in equal measure. Turnbull had a long if spotty history of involvement with the party, first running for Wentworth pre-selection in 1981 and losing to Peter Costello's father-in-law, Peter Coleman, who had the support of Malcolm Fraser. However, he lacked the tribal commitment to the Liberals that so many party members valued. The fact that he wasn't associated with a single political philosophy other than the vague nationalism of the Australian Republican Movement could have been a great strength. The most successful Liberal Party leaders have combined general liberal and conservative principles with a ruthless pragmatism in their implementation. He showed with the

ARM a willingness to fight for something he believed in but didn't show much in the way of pragmatism. Turnbull's role in the republic debate showed his strengths and weaknesses. His energy, advocacy skills and financial resources had helped the ARM get closer to their goal than could have been imagined when that group was formed in 1991. Yet his dismissive attitude towards those contemplating a directly elected president helped to prevent a united republican movement in 1999. One republican from outside the ARM orbit, Tim Costello, recalled, 'When you're on the wrong end of Malcolm it's terrifying, the thunder in the face.' On the night of the referendum loss, Turnbull underlined his remarkable ability to burn bridges by putting the blame on John Howard. Still, he had the support of Howard in his pre-selection, and in his rapid ascension to cabinet.[5] Howard was secure enough in his own position to promote future leadership prospects, though subsequent leaders have found this more difficult. The style of Turnbull's pre-selection in Wentworth didn't endear him to others in the party. Backbenchers hated the precedent of a sitting member being challenged. The incumbent Peter King was a moderate, the dominant faction in New South Wales. Yet Abbott worked overtime to try to block Turnbull's rise into the ranks of the parliamentary Liberal Party, communicating with Wentworth Liberals who were monarchists, telling them of the dangers Turnbull posed to the parliamentary party.

Turnbull's enthusiasm in welcoming Barack Obama's victory in the American presidential election shortly after he was elected leader in 2008 was a sign that Turnbull was a fundamentally progressive figure in a conservative party. 'Barack Obama's victory is more than the realisation of Martin Luther King's dream,' he said. 'It is also the opportunity for a stronger America, with a new leader, to take up the call of Dr King to "let freedom ring" around the world.' Where Howard had drawn accusations of interfering in American democracy when he claimed early in 2007 that a victory for Obama would be a victory for al-Qaeda, Turnbull was comfortable with the Illinois senator's win. Journalists eventually drew Turnbull into an explicit repudiation of Howard's remarks.

Kevin Rudd, whose own distance from his party would cost him his leadership, needled the new opposition leader in parliament about his lack of attachment to his party. 'We have a lot in common,' Rudd said in Question Time. 'We both knocked off sitting Liberal MPs. Both of us spent many years seeking Labor Party pre-selection. And neither of us have killed a cat, have we, Malcolm?' The latter jibe referred to a much-traversed story about a girlfriend of Turnbull's, after she gave young Mal the flick, finding her deceased feline on the front doorstep. Turnbull twice sued newspaper columnists who labelled him a cat-killer. 'No cat has died at my hands,' he told Annabel Crabb.

As academic and TV presenter Waleed Aly has pointed out, factionalism in the Liberal Party correlates almost perfectly with views on climate change.[6] As opposition leader, Turnbull had made a conservative appeal to climate-change sceptics, arguing that action on carbon abatement was a smart risk-management strategy, and invoking Margaret Thatcher as an early greenhouse warrior. Turnbull wasn't going to convince the denialists, though, whose position was as much about adversarial cultural politics as science. Nick Minchin revealed this attitude on a *Four Corners* interview that was a signal to more junior figures to speak out. Minchin pronounced climate change a giant conspiracy. 'For the extreme left, it provides the opportunity to do what they have always wanted to do, which is to sort of de-industrialise the Western world,' he claimed. 'The collapse of communism was a disaster for the left and, really, they embraced environment as their new religion.' Whether Minchin believed this or not, it galvanised his side of the debate. Conservatives drew on support from Liberal Party rank-and-file members to combat Turnbull's position on climate change.

The contrast of Turnbull's position as an advocate for action on climate change with that of another conservative moderniser, Britain's David Cameron, is instructive. Donning a green outfit distinguished Cameron most clearly as a modern politician after taking on the leadership of the Conservative Party in 2005. Turnbull shared Cameron's position as a progressive leader of a party whose grassroots members were much more conservative than the electorate. Cameron had the advantage, though, of taking the leadership after three election losses and three failed opposition leaders. The parliamentary party, at that point, will swallow almost anything if it gets them onto the Treasury benches. MPs are younger with fewer ties to the previous period of government. As Howard found in 1995, by that point even long-term political enemies can be persuaded to concentrate their attack on the government. As Turnbull later discovered, the desperation level of MPs in government can also make them do the unthinkable. Not desperate enough, though, to give him much licence on policy.

One of the things Turnbull had done in the six years since losing the leadership to Abbott in 2009 was to attempt to build relationships across the party. It was less than a month into his prime ministership, though, when Turnbull was shown that some parts of his party would not forgive him for deposing Abbott in 2015. He addressed the NSW Liberal Party State Council, the home division of both men. 'We are not run by factions,' Turnbull said. This statement was met with laughter and groans from parts of the audience. 'Well, you may dispute that, but I have to tell you, from experience, we are not run by factions, nor are we run by big business, or by deals in back rooms. We rely on the ideas and the energy and enterprise of our membership.' Under normal circumstances, this would be Liberal Party boilerplate designed to contrast the party's organisation with Labor's more managed factions. In light of what had happened in previous months, it was a tone-deaf performance for the new leader. It would be one of a number of occasions in the months after taking the job when Turnbull was either poorly advised or impervious to good advice. At the same time a moderate push to dominate pre-selection showdowns in New South Wales was headed off by prime-ministerial intervention to prevent factional warfare detracting from the government's performance. However, in the months that followed, an all-out factional brawl erupted as the pre-selection showdowns for the 2016 election were opened.

The conservatives within the Liberal Party, including the former prime minister, flexed their collective political muscles at the beginning of the 2016 election year. Their goal was to prevent Turnbull from transforming the historical conservatism of the party, even if under new leadership the Coalition was successful at the election. Turnbull knew that the party membership at the organisational level is more conservative than him. The parliamentary membership is largely careerist and prone to support whoever they think can win an election, but the conservative voices know that they can loudly announce their disagreements with government policy, especially from the backbench, to rouse the membership. This tempers any internal efforts to embrace progressive ideas, because the subsequent public disunity can harm leaders. Having removed Abbott on the pledge to make the party more competitive in the polls, Turnbull was to some extent beholden to these same backbenchers. This created a tension between the need to continue appealing to new voters, especially younger voters, and the reality that the base of support for the Liberal Party represents an older demographic.[7]

The delcon phenomenon was not a matter of a fight between Abbott and his supporters and Turnbull and his supporters. Turnbull didn't really have many supporters in the sense that the likes of Howard, Peacock and Costello had their 'spear carriers'—as they are known in the Liberal Party. Sinodinos came closest to this description but he had limited experience of politics from within the parliamentary ranks. The left of the party would have happily coalesced around somebody other than Turnbull if the right leader had emerged. Conversely, antipathy towards Turnbull helped Abbott take the leadership in 2009, and sustained him early in 2015 when so many backbenchers were critical of his performance. The drawn-out leadership battle left many scars.

The past is prologue, though, and political sins can be forgiven. That is where Turnbull's personality comes in. Had he paid his more conservative colleagues the respect they thought they deserved as elected MPs, party office holders, ministers and shadow ministers, his first experience of the party leadership might have lasted longer than 500 days, and the delcon phenomenon might have been avoided once Abbott's weaknesses became clear. Arrogance is hardly a scarce commodity in politics. Leaders need to find the right balance between humility and self-confidence. Howard might have been grating in his declaration of the former trait but that is better than the lack of self-awareness that more arrogant leaders display. Still, Turnbull has a record of cultivating good relations with conservative figures in the party. He had befriended Alexander Downer, still an influential figure when Turnbull was opposition leader. On the other hand, Peter Costello and Turnbull typify the relationship between personalities and ideas that make factionalism in the party complicated. Although Turnbull was more genuinely liberal in his outlook, he and Costello promised similar policy trajectories, continuing Howard's economic policies while modernising the Liberal Party's approach to social and environmental issues, as well as the constitution. But they couldn't stand each other. The fact that many moderates clung to Costello was mostly about their antipathy towards Howard. Howard is often said to have turned the Liberal Party into a conservative rather than a liberal organisation. The faces of the parliamentary party at state and federal level, though, tell a different story. The fact that Turnbull was a good fit for the moderate wing was a sign of how much that group's taste for economic intervention had receded since the 1980s.

One of the better relationships Turnbull had with conservative MPs was with immigration minister Peter Dutton, but only after a rocky start when Turnbull became prime minister. This may be Turnbull's best example of pragmatism dictating his relations with an important player in his orbit who he wouldn't naturally get along with. Turnbull—in spite of perceptions of his relationship with Dutton when he removed him from the National Security Committee on the advice of Sinodinos (a mistake Turnbull corrected after the election)—went out of his way to court Dutton as leader of the conservative bloc in the ministry. Not exactly a pigeon pair when it comes to interests, Dutton was not the sort of colleague to whom Turnbull normally showed respect. Dutton has endured Turnbull's temper, as have many others. But the former detective isn't easily intimidated, and experience has taught him that when Turnbull vents his frustration it's a reflection of the pressure he's under, not some intractable divide. Turnbull allies would do well to learn this lesson so as to minimise fallouts. Dutton is an important sounding board for Turnbull in the aftermath of the election, because as the senior right-wing figure in cabinet he is Turnbull's best chance of maintaining unity where it matters—among conservatives more interested in electoral success with policy outcomes than retribution and failure because someone more liberal than them is leading the party. How this relationship endures will be an important test as to whether the Turnbull gamble pays off beyond scraping home at the election.

Another group of conservatives whom Turnbull needed to court had less personal antipathy to him but was even more distant from the leader in policy terms. The role of the National Party underlines Turnbull's institutional limitations on modernising his government, another reason to doubt Turnbull's capacity to shift the cultural lines on the right of politics. It was Mark Twain who once said reports of his death had been greatly exaggerated. So it has been with the Nationals, written off by academics and journalists alike for years. As the proportion of Australians living on the land has declined, the Nationals have changed their strategy, placing more focus on regional town centres and coastal communities. The switch to Turnbull was seen as a boon for the government in the cities, much more so than the regions. Turnbull was forced to recognise that without the Nationals exceeding expectations at the election, he wouldn't have retained the prime ministership. Yet, while few Nationals share Turnbull's liberalism, the party can be dealt with—unlike the delcons—on a rational transactional basis. That problem was solidified by the election result, where the Nationals gained Liberal Sharman Stone's seat of Murray and increased their representation in the House of Representatives, while the Liberals went backwards. They did this in part by running a campaign with a different emphasis than that of the Liberals, since Turnbull's liberal approach to both the economy and social issues was not popular with the Nationals' constituency. Nationals thus improved their representation on Turnbull's frontbench, as per the Coalition agreement.

The Liberals and Nationals have always had an uneasy alliance. John Howard as prime minister understood the importance of bringing the Nationals with him after having presided over a split in the Coalition during his first stint as Liberal leader ahead of the 1987 election. In government he used the proceeds of the mining boom to invest in regional projects to pacify Nationals about such policy scripts as gun reform and the introduction of the GST. He also ensured Nationals were well represented on the government's frontbench, earning brownie points for not downgrading the role of his junior Coalition partner after the 1996 victory, the size of which could have seen the Liberals govern in their own right. Nationals during the Howard years received the lion's share of the credit for regional projects the Coalition embarked on, sometimes to the irritation of regional Liberal MPs.

Nationals haven't always been on the same ideological page as the Liberal Party, certainly not in the modern era. 'Agrarian socialists' is the deliberately disparaging way some Liberals like to describe their junior Coalition partner. While the replacement of Abbott by Turnbull improved the government's fortunes in the cities, no such upswing was seen in regional areas, serving to heighten the potential for disagreements between the two parties. When the Coalition wins in a landslide, as it did in 2013, it tends to do proportionately better in the cities and therefore in Liberal seats. For the Nationals to hold their seats while One Nation was again on the march in their heartland was potentially even worse news for Turnbull, since deputy PM Barnaby Joyce's populism would only become entrenched in order to see off the Hanson revival. Joyce destroyed independent Tony Windsor in their showdown in New England, winning a majority of the primary vote and navigating a path for the Nationals different from Turnbull's difficult-to-sell 'jobs and growth' slogan, using a ground campaign around the country to retain seats many pundits had given up on. But there is opportunity for Turnbull in the rise of the Nationals. If the relationship between Turnbull and Joyce can be successfully managed it provides a compelling contrast that just might draw in constituencies each man on his own would otherwise repel. But the premise is that their relationship needs to be close.

When he was left out of the Turnbull ministry in 2015, Turnbull's friend and former cabinet minister Ian Macfarlane announced his intention to join the National Party caucus, which under the Coalition agreement would have allowed the Nationals an additional cabinet portfolio. Macfarlane's move was blocked by the state Liberal National Party organisation but not before speculation about subsequent defections destabilised the government and put the new prime minister on notice not to take his rural representatives for granted. This episode underlined the extent to which tribalism and personal ambition can dominate conservative politics. After the election the number of National Party representatives in the ministry was once again up for discussion. Joyce described the matter as a case of 'simple arithmetic', and so it was with the Nationals growing their representation in the cabinet, and being in a position to demand that the small-business portfolio go to a newly appointed National in the outer ministry. The Nationals also expected a greater say on some social policies. The contrast between the efficient way the Nationals did business after the election with the way the delcons carried on their personal crusade is instructive.

Some conservative partisans find governing a frustrating process, full of compromises and chasing middle-of-the-road votes. They find opposition cathartic, a chance to bring out their tribalism and throw insults at the Labor Party, but also at their supposed colleagues. The 'primal scream' of the delcons, as one cabinet minister described it to us, would continue up to and beyond the election campaign. Every poor decision Turnbull took, and there would be more than a few, could be expected to be accompanied by anonymous briefing from within the party and by hostile commentary from the delcon columnists. It is hard to know where the delcons plan to take their anger at Turnbull, or if they even have a plan. Abbott is a very unlikely candidate for a comeback—and as the delcon candidate of choice that must frustrate them. But, of course, they probably don't accept just how unrealistic an Abbott comeback is. Dutton is no friend of the delcons, using the terminology to describe them privately. He might be the unofficial leader of the right, but you don't take on such status and be deluded enough to think the delcons are representative. Christian Porter and Josh Frydenberg are of a similar mind. Angus Taylor is cited almost as often by delcons as a future conservative leader as Taylor himself likes to put his Oxford education to use and cite Edmund Burke as the model of a conservative who wasn't a hard-right fringe dweller. The most likely outcome is that the delcons will continue to rail against Turnbull, hurt him when doing so, but discredit themselves more so in the wider electorate. Because commentators dominate the delcon ranks, their collective failure to understand parliamentary realities won't much matter. They have a platform and they will keep on using it. Not to attract people to their position, but to outlast opponents and use their survival to claim victory. This is the state of modern Australian politics, and what Turnbull would be facing as he headed into the 2016 election campaign.

Five
DOUBLING DOWN

THE MOMENTS THAT define political careers tend to be the big decisions—whether about policy or political strategy. John Howard always discussed his biggest decisions with his family, his close advisers and his cabinet (although the latter wasn't always the first port of call). A defining element of Howard's success was the bitter experience of his first stint as leader when consultation wasn't a strength. Consultation matters. Consultation not just with those whose opinions he valued, but with the wider backbench as well. The *appearance* of consultation was just as important to Howard as the decisions it produced. Consultation also gave Howard a strong sense of where MPs stood on a range of issues and how they felt about him. Tony Abbott observed this leadership style as a Howard favourite but failed to practise it even after colleagues were quite explicit about this weakness during the failed spill vote in early 2015. Consultation with his parliamentary colleagues would be crucial to Malcolm Turnbull's survival, given both his natural tendency to alienate them with an imperious style and the need to improve his political judgement, which had been wanting during Utegate and the ETS negotiations with Rudd in 2008–09.

Turnbull had never been especially consultative, with the exception of the close counsel he kept with his wife, Lucy. They had worked together on the *Spycatcher* trial. She also brought the political pedigree of the Hughes family—her father, Tom Hughes, was attorney-general in the Gorton and McMahon governments. Although her political instincts are more social democratic than those of her husband, in her absence, Turnbull has often cited his wife's opinion as an authority. Lucy made her views known on policy issues and frontbench positions. In this respect Turnbull and Howard had more in common than either man might be willing to admit. But the dynamics of the first couples are different. Janette Howard wasn't a policy boffin in the way that Lucy Turnbull is. Equally, Mrs Turnbull's political instincts aren't as well refined as Mrs Howard's were. This left Turnbull in an interesting position. His team of advisers needed to be all that they could be when offering political advice, and if their advice contradicted that of Lucy, the risk for the new prime minister was that he would side with his wife. When Howard had done this it was often to his advantage. For Turnbull the advantage was far from guaranteed. Prime ministers get their way more often on political judgements than policy pronouncements, which tend to go through a more formal process, the latter being Lucy's biggest strength.

Turnbull's biggest problem when selecting staff has long been that if he picks up advisers with 'political' experience, he invariably disrespects their credibility beyond the narrow world of politics. But if he finds talent outside the political ranks, while Turnbull is happy at first, he quickly turns on the staffers, pointing out that their lack of political know-how is problematic. Neither model of staffer works. Overall, the Turnbull circle of advice narrowed once he became prime minister. His office was inexperienced, and the distrust with the Abbott camp, which meant the corporate memory from one office to the next was lost, was a problem. Tales of the wreckage left after an all-night wake in the Prime Minister's Offices on the night of the leadership vote speaks to the disdain those leaving had for the team about to move in.

When the party room met to discuss the fallout from the change of prime minister, Turnbull made a point of telling colleagues that he had employed a 'doorstop' at the entrance to the media office of the PMO, as a symbolic gesture that the door is never closed to those seeking to offer advice or find out answers. The wedge is apparently still at the entrance, but whether or not the symbolism was ever matched by reality is a contested proposition among Turnbull's colleagues.

In the midst of the distrust passing from one office to the next, weakening opinion polls and a closing circle of advice, Turnbull had to make his biggest political decision yet—whether or not to test his support at a double-dissolution election. Doing so would require an early and longer than usual election campaign—in order to align the houses and secure the passage of Senate reforms and industrial relations legislation designed to be the trigger. It was a risky way to start a campaign.

One of Turnbull's favourite words—'optionality'—is business jargon that emphasises leaving open as many opportunities as possible by not making decisions until the last possible moment. There is something to be said for leaving room to move in politics. In *Battleground* we criticised Tony Abbott's muscular rhetoric for increasing his path dependence—leaving the electorate clear about his position but leaving himself little room to change his mind. We can see Turnbull's embrace of optionality in the tax debate, where it didn't seem to do him much good but probably produced the right political decision in not going to the election promising to increase the GST. In election timing, too, Turnbull had a few options. His preference was to run a full term, with an election in August or September 2016. There was no shortage of advice—Senator Scott Ryan wanted the latest possible date, advice Arthur Sinodinos was sympathetic to. When Christopher Pyne's preference for a snap election before Christmas was rejected, he argued for March. Election timing was influenced by delays in changing the Senate electoral system. The minister in charge of electoral affairs, Mathias Cormann, convinced Turnbull at a private meeting in February that a double dissolution in July would give the government enough time to change the electoral system without looking like they were hanging on until the last possible moment. As one cabinet minister told us, 'the Senate reform tail wagged the election timing dog'.

Turnbull told his first cabinet as chair that the decision to remove Abbott was purely pragmatic, not ideological, which both made sense and left those hoping for an ideological change of direction disappointed. While plans to remove Abbott were kept under wraps, there was a view by Team Turnbull that once the move was on it wouldn't be a hard thing to make happen. As a cabinet minister told us, by September 2015 Turnbull was an 'irresistible force confronting a readily moveable object'. Scott Morrison was far more involved in the coup than he ever let on, speaking with Turnbull over the phone immediately after the February spill motion to plan out where to go from there. Yet once the deal was done and Morrison was ensconced as treasurer, he was somewhat of a marginalised figure, at least by the right. While the broader right had little time for the delcons, they still blamed Morrison for acting in a way that was unbecoming of someone who sought to be a future right-wing candidate for the leadership. Morrison would have to immediately succeed in the treasury portfolio to win supporters back to his banner. That hasn't happened. One of the barriers to Morrison's rise is the 'Hockey club', as Pyne has dubbed it. The club is represented by a cross-factional group who once supported Joe Hockey as the next big thing in Liberal politics. It included Peter Dutton, Steve Ciobo, Jamie Briggs—who of course is no longer in parliament—Michael Keenan and even the finance minister Mathias Cormann. Once Hockey was out of the picture this group dispersed, but retained their disdain for Morrison.

During the nine months Turnbull was PM leading up to the 2016 election, the right within his party were convinced that he would walk away from the plebiscite on same-sex marriage. This misread the anger that had permeated the party at the way Abbott had handled the party-room discussion on the subject. Turnbull knew he couldn't change position on this issue. In fact, some of his supporters, such as backbencher Craig Laundy, made their support conditional on Turnbull's keeping the plebiscite. Eventually, these issues faded into the background on the eve of the calling of the election, although the question of whether conservatives would respect a popular vote over same-sex marriage did come back into the debate just ahead of polling day, unhelpfully for Turnbull.

Double Disillusionment

By 2016, it had been nearly thirty years since Australia experienced a double-dissolution election. The provision in the Australian constitution to break a deadlock between the two Houses of Parliament had been used on occasion prior to 1987 for a variety of reasons. Only once, in 1974, has a double dissolution been followed by a joint sitting of parliament to pass the contested bills. More often, this election trigger has been used to hold an election at a time of the prime minister's choosing. The reason this has become comparatively rare is that doubling the number of senators up for election halves the quota required for a seat, from 14.3 to 7.7 per cent of the statewide vote, providing small parties a greater chance of representation.[1] Combined with the effect of the increase in the number of senators from ten to twelve in each state in 1984, the quota for election at a double-dissolution election puts seats within reach of the ragtag minor parties that make passing legislation unpredictable for governments.

After the 2013 Senate result, when 'micro-parties' swapping preferences delivered seats to the likes of the Motoring Enthusiast Party with a primary vote of 0.5 per cent, the Joint Standing Committee on Electoral Matters recommended changes to the Senate voting system. The bipartisan recommendation, to adopt the system of optional preferential voting similar to that already in place in the New South Wales upper house, raised little public discussion outside preference-whispering circles. At a half-Senate election, a party would in all likelihood need more than 5 per cent of the primary vote to reach the threshold of over 14 per cent. Not so at a double-dissolution election.

However, by the time the government was prepared to give effect to this recommendation, Labor refused to support the legislation so the government negotiated with the Greens. While the Greens like to portray themselves as above the power machinations of the 'old parties', as an incumbent party they were more than happy to slam the door to the Senate shut to smaller challengers. The micro-parties may have been an irritant to the major parties but they were direct competitors to the Greens. Yet the Greens appeared blindsided by the double-dissolution election, lost a seat and came close to losing more. During the debate over the bills, Labor senators made all sorts of sanctimonious arguments against the supposed undemocratic nature of the proposed system; it seems more likely that after the Senate report Labor's number crunchers found a disadvantage for the party in the optional preferential mechanism. Making below-the-line voting easier reduced the power of factions, as Tasmanian Lisa Singh showed when she won the fifth Labor seat from sixth position on Labor's list. It led to the embarrassing situation for Labor that it was going against the express advice of its shadow electoral matters spokesperson, Gary Gray. In fact Gray had argued internally that the electoral advantage from the reforms was more likely to benefit Labor than the Coalition. But he was rolled by Stephen Conroy with the support of Bill Shorten, with the pair arguing that taking a position that endeared them to the crossbenchers was the better way to go because it would be useful in turning them against the government, to cause maximum damage to the Coalition's agenda. Gray thought it was very short-sighted, and at the expense of doing what represented good reform with good political advantage for Labor in the long run. The West Australian MP was retiring at the looming election anyway, so rather than abide by the shadow cabinet decision, Gray chose to resign and stand firm. Mathias Cormann, who had taken over responsibility as special minister of state under

Turnbull, adding the portfolio to his finance duties, tried to exploit the divisions in Labor's ranks but there were bigger issues on the national agenda, so he got little traction.

If Turnbull wanted a mid-year election, convinced to break from his long-preferred option of going full term, it would have to be in July and it would have to be a double dissolution. Such an election would have to be called within six months of the expiry of the House of Representatives on 11 May. But senators elected before the end of June would have their terms backdated to the previous July. This would in turn necessitate a half-Senate election within two years, or a Senate-only election—which hadn't happened since the early 1970s. This was the reason for the early election in 1984, following the March 1983 double dissolution called by Malcolm Fraser. An election called in early May for a polling day in early July would mean a long campaign, such as Bob Hawke instigated in 1984. The similarities were a bad omen for Turnbull, with Hawke having done poorly even against a hapless opposition leader in Andrew Peacock. Turnbull could have waited for a half-Senate election to become constitutional in August. Turnbull's mistake was not acting as the autocrat he is so often labelled as. Rather, he listened to the advice of those around him. The danger for the Turnbull gamble succeeding beyond scraping home at the July 2016 election is that a wounded PM learns the wrong lesson. That he closes his mind to advice, rather than becomes more discerning in the advice he chooses to follow.

A double dissolution was at cross purposes with the intention of the changes to Senate voting. Observers closely watch the lower house for the risk of a hung parliament, but—with the recent exception of the final term of the Howard government—numbers in the Senate are always more evenly balanced. The danger for the government after the election was that having won the campaign and therefore earning a mandate for its policies in the lower house, the Senate would be just as unwieldy as the one that stared down Abbott. On the other hand, a half-Senate election in August or September under the new voting rules would improve things a bit. Independent senator John Madigan was up for re-election and would have little chance of surviving under the new rules. A double dissolution would also end the terms of chancers such as Dio Wang and Glenn Lazarus, elected on Clive Palmer's coat-tails. However, they would in all likelihood be replaced by a crossbench just as unpredictable. Labor could hardly be blamed for matching Abbott's obstructionism. What no one in the government seriously considered at this time was the risk of unleashing the One Nation phenomenon on the federal parliament, exactly twenty years after Pauline Hanson was first elected. Hanson was paid for a regular spot on *Sunrise* when she should have been paying for the publicity.

South Australian independent senator Nick Xenophon had won almost two quotas in 2013 but his running mate had been frozen out of preference exchanges. The lower quota, and with Xenophon himself again at the top of the ticket, guaranteed the anti-gambling campaigner three Senate seats. The double dissolution also transformed Tasmanian independent Jacqui Lambie, who first entered the Senate in Clive Palmer's party, from an outside chance to a near certainty for re-election. One Nation won four seats in total. Three NXT senators, South Australian Bob Day, David Leyonjhelm, Lambie and Derryn Hinch added to a broad crossbench. The government would need the support of nine of eleven crossbenchers if Labor and the Greens were 'No' votes. The double dissolution was partly a matter of Turnbull's preferred timing. As is often the case with Turnbull, he was a man in a hurry. But it was launched on advice.

To prepare for a July election, Turnbull needed to line up a series of preconditions. A double dissolution under the existing Senate voting system would produce any number of micro-parties so he needed the Greens to agree to pass the legislation in a marathon session that saw the Senate sit for twenty-eight consecutive hours. Nick Xenophon even made an appearance in his pyjamas. Labor and the Greens kept most of their venom for each other—Labor senators objecting to the parliamentary procedures used to pass the legislation and needling the Greens about their priorities in advancing changes to the voting system while political donation reform languished.

The budget would have to be moved forward a week to allow time for supply bills to be passed before the election campaign so that the public service could be paid. While this might have been done quickly after the election, there was no margin for error. Moving the budget forward at the last minute added to the messy optics, especially when it appeared that the treasurer was one of the last senior figures in the broader leadership group to be informed of the plans. Then, Turnbull needed to make a show of the parliament rejecting legislation for a second time. A trigger had been available to the government since 2014, when the Senate twice rejected legislation to abolish the Clean Energy Finance Corporation. However, industrial relations measures might galvanise the Coalition behind Turnbull's leadership going into the campaign.

Considering the heat generated by the 2014 budget, it was surprising that only one of the contested measures had provided a trigger for a double dissolution. Drawing attention to unpopular measures like deregulating university fees was not a smart election strategy in any event. Instead, Turnbull relied on a more familiar Coalition talking point. The Registered Organisations legislation had already been blocked twice but Turnbull wanted a stronger justification for his actions. The Australian Building and Construction Commission had been established by the Howard government and abolished by the Rudd government. It was Coalition policy at the 2013 election. The word 'prorogue' made a welcome return to the national lexicon as Turnbull asked the governor-general to end the parliamentary sitting, then in recess, clearing the way for a special sitting in late April to consider the ABCC bill. The Commonwealth parliament had not been prorogued since 1977, and then only to allow for a ceremonial opening of parliament by the Queen. The strategy was devised by the attorney-general, George Brandis, and he delighted in the way that it caught Labor and most of the commentariat off guard.

Turnbull didn't have strong feelings about the substance of the ABCC legislation, as unimpressed with the civil-liberties infringements it contained as he was with the union thuggery that supposedly justified the body. Nor did he expect the special sitting to pass the bill, and there was very little else for parliament to do other than to make trouble for the government, by, for example, calling Arthur Sinodinos to appear before a Senate committee investigating dodgy political fundraising. The NSW Electoral Commission embarrassed the cabinet secretary when it withheld $4.4 million in public funding on the basis that the party had disguised the identity of prohibited donors. Sinodinos had been finance director of the NSW Liberal Division during the 2011 state campaign. He had been called as a witness before the Independent Commission Against Corruption and the question of whether he should be stood down pending the commission's recommendations became a sore point between Sinodinos and the office of then Prime Minister Abbott, sending John Howard's long-time chief of staff further into the arms of Turnbull's campaign to unseat Abbott. Sinodinos eventually refused to appear but the issues gained another airing and Turnbull learned, not for the last time, what a complex and unpredictable set of events he was putting in train.

The Numbers

In past decades, the task facing Turnbull in getting a first-term government re-elected would not have been a great one. While the Hawke and Howard governments had suffered significant swings against them after difficult first parliaments, they went on to improve their standing at subsequent elections. A first-term government had not fallen since the 1930s. Yet Labor had come close under Gillard in 2010, and Abbott had been turfed out as leader primarily because of doubts about his ability to learn from his mistakes and regain his ascendancy over Labor in time for the coming election. Perennially nervous backbenchers had seen first-term governments fall in Victoria in 2014 and Queensland in early 2015, shortly before the first spill motion against Abbott. They remained anxious when, after the February 'near death experience' for Abbott, he showed little signs of changing his style, and the gap in the polls remained.

A more liberal figure such as Turnbull would gather votes in different places than Abbott, so the theory went. If he would have less appeal in the outer suburbs and regional areas, though, it wasn't clear where Turnbull would make up the difference. Seats such as Reid in Sydney's inner west, held by Turnbull supporter Craig Laundy, would be easier to defend. Picking up similar ethnically diverse seats would be difficult, however, if the likes of Lindsay in the outer west were to fall. Quite different issues motivated constituents in these relatively nearby electorates. The Liberals also ended up taking the eastern Melbourne seat of Chisholm from Labor and made moves towards one day being competitive in Rudd's former seat of Griffith in Brisbane.

Complicating this picture even more was the long-term dealignment of voters from the major parties. John Howard observed that when he first campaigned for the Liberal Party in the 1960s, the major parties had bedrock support of 40 per cent each and would compete for the remaining voters. Some of those voters would ally themselves to a party for a number of elections, allowing one party to build a temporary coalition. As prime minister, Howard said the ratio was more like 30:30:40.[2] This was probably an overestimate of unaligned voters at the time but close to the situation in 2016. Political scientists measure this effect by asking voters whether they identify with a political party. Fewer voters say they do than was the case in the 1960s but the number for the major parties has stabilised at about 35 per cent each in the last few elections. The biggest fall in very strong party identification—these are the 'rusted on' voters—has been on Labor's side. In the past Labor could rely on 40 per cent of the electorate voting for them without even campaigning. In recent elections, though, this group has fallen as low as 16 per cent. That is why Labor has become so good at campaigning. It has had to in order to survive.[3]

In line with this trend, more and more voters have started making up their minds whom to support late in campaigns. Around a quarter of voters reported considering changing their vote during the campaign. Part of this phenomenon involves voters taking seriously their civic responsibility and listening to what leaders have to say even if they don't end up changing their vote. These are not necessarily swinging voters, but it can be impossible for parties to target swinging voters because they often don't pay much attention to politics. They often vote only because it's compulsory. The trends Howard cited, then, have made campaigns increasingly complex. Labor cottoned onto this trend in modern politics well before the Coalition did, shifting its focus to direct messaging via robo calls—automatically generated messages to landline and mobile telephone numbers discussing issues targeted at particular voters, sometimes left by prominent political identities who start by introducing themselves—which were more likely to pierce through to voters who otherwise weren't reading the mainstream press or listening to advertising.

The tracking polling by the major parties, which targets individual electorates with candidate names, substantially ramps up during election campaigns. It uses rolling small sample sizes across five days, dropping the earliest day off and replacing it with the most recent to give the party strategists a sense of how their message is being received in the marginal seats, as well as how it is evolving as the campaign progresses. A Labor campaign worker added that because most published polls use landlines instead of mobiles there are increasing doubts about their accuracy. Track polling covers key seats on a rolling five- or seven-day series of surveys that can be assessed as a whole, or broken down into individual contests to gauge momentum and party standing in targeted seats. Electorates can drop in and out of the wider track as new information comes to hand. Party research was crucial to the so-called sandbagging of seats by the Coalition, alongside Labor's efforts to target electorates it could pick off one by one in an attempt to build its 55 seats won at the 2013 election into 76 or more seats to secure a majority.

Knowing where limited resources needed to be deployed was crucial for the Coalition to outgun Labor in the seats that mattered. 'There is nothing wrong with a swing against us, as long as it's smaller than the margin of the seats we hold,' one Liberal close to the action told us. The government hoped its sandbagging strategy—targeting resources at key seats that were necessary for retaining a majority even when the nationwide vote was slipping in safe seats held by either major party—would work in unison with the popularity of local MPs, including first-terms MPs fighting to retain seats won at the last election. These MPs often benefit from the fact that they have vanquished a popular local member at the previous election. Facing a novice MP in the next contest, they enjoy a 'sophomore surge'.

Both sides ramped up resources in contests they believed they could win, and pulled out of those that the internal polling told them were lost. In Labor's case this meant it was targeting less than the additional 21 seats it needed on top of the 55 won at the 2013 election in order to form majority government. This was an especially hard process for marginal-seat MPs on the Coalition side to accept. Because the Coalition won big in 2013, it was the conservatives who went through this process in 2016, as the strategists ruled a line under Liberal seats such as Dobell and Paterson in New South Wales.

Some local MPs liked to think their personal following was enormous. Even a 2 or 3 per cent advantage could be decisive, especially when an opposition was trying to pick up 21 seats to form majority government. With the odd exception where a sitting MP was retiring or a new seat had been constituted, this meant the opposition had to overcome nearly two dozen marginal-seat MPs fighting for their political lives if it wanted to build a working majority. That's tough. It's one reason why we have only had seven changes of government since World War II.

The shift in modern campaigning away from defined mainstream media boundaries to a wide array of online journalism and social media interest put enormous pressure on the parties to avoid mistakes, right at the time when full costings were being released and advertising blackouts taking effect. It also meant strategists couldn't afford to miss trends, as the Coalition did in Tasmania. All three Liberal-held seats being unexpectedly lost there was the difference between Turnbull being hailed a hero and a failure by sections of the Liberal Party. Had these three seats been retained, as expected, along with a few dozen votes going the other way in Herbert, the Coalition would have had a comfortable majority, leaving only the likes of the delcons to lament the PM's electoral performance.

Before the 2016 election, the Coalition held 90 seats in the 150-member House of Representatives, Labor had 55 seats and crossbenchers held the 5 remaining seats. The magic number to form government with a majority is 76 seats, a figure only formally confirmed for Turnbull on Monday 11 July, more than a week after the election. Redistributions and new seats changed the notional configuration of the parliament, moving Labor's target to 20 seats. While Labor performed well at the election, it never seriously entertained winning enough seats to secure a majority in its own right. In the end it fell 7 seats short.

Before entering politics, Labor's assistant treasury spokesman at the election, Andrew Leigh, was an Australian National University professor of economics. He co-wrote an academic paper highlighting the accurate predictions of the betting agencies when compared with polling evidence.[4] When the election was called one major betting agency predicted the Coalition would retain 80 seats, with Labor winning 66. Betting markets are said to be accurate because they are dominated by those with inside knowledge of politics. Gamblers' confidence in a Coalition win marked a contrast with opinion polls showing a close contest in which Labor had nosed ahead. However, Shorten's populist rhetoric was likely to galvanise Labor voters without guaranteeing success in marginal seats. National polls do not factor in individual contests between sometimes popular local MPs and candidates. These usually favour incumbents, with their ability to pork-barrel and leverage the advantages of MPs with local offices and a generous postal allowance. This was how John Howard won the 1998 election with just 48.9 per cent of the national two-party vote. Bob Hawke did the same in 1990, defeating Andrew Peacock's opposition Coalition with less than 50 per cent of the national vote. In 2016 Labor's clever Medicare scare campaign considerably eroded the Coalition's incumbency advantage. Another important factor eroding the Coalition's incumbency advantage was self-inflicted. Postage and printing allowances are allocated per financial year, and because the election was called for 2 July most MPs and senators had reached their maximums in advance of the campaign. Had the election been held in the second half of the year after the allowances reset, or indeed earlier as Christopher Pyne had pushed for, Coalition incumbents would have had a far greater resource advantage over their opponents in individual key seats. This was a factor Liberal strategists we spoke to emphasised and a significant factor behind the party's failure to retain more of the seats targeted for sandbagging.

Bill Shorten's problem was that he didn't cut an inspiring figure as a leader in the campaign—opposition leaders rarely do. Exceptions to the rule, such as Kevin Rudd's 2007 campaign, usually occur in the context of opposition leaders taking on long-term governments or prime ministers, or both. Shorten was able, though, to transfer his skills as negotiator in the union movement to a transactional style of political leadership. He didn't seek to inspire on the policy front, although the volume of policy he released prior to the campaign was notable. Shorten simply wanted voters to believe that he would give them a better deal when it came to looking after their health and the education of their children. Pulling at heartstrings but with a transactional solution: more money to improve outcomes. It was a delicate transactional play, because it butted up against the Coalition's claim that Labor would blow the budget.

Just as Labor couldn't vacate the economic debate, Turnbull would struggle with Abbott's legacy on health and education—in the realms of both policy and trust. Hence the government's attempt to frame both issues in terms of economic management: more money didn't necessarily mean better outcomes, especially if the extra funds came at the long-term expense of balancing the books. But such issues could be managed, so Liberals thought. Their collective worry was how Turnbull would hold up in the campaign. He was always at risk of derailing, some within the Coalition's ranks thought. Turnbull's first stint as leader revealed a penchant for jumping at shadows, and a lack of electioneering experience if things got tight would lump even more pressure on an unproven campaigner. Turnbull must have come across the derailing concept in his extensive business dealings, but that didn't make him immune from falling victim to it. One of Shorten's few obvious strengths in his match-up with Turnbull was his battle-hardened experience from his time as a union official. Union campaigns get nasty, which suggested Shorten knew how to take hits and deliver them. Not enough Liberal planning went into preparing for just how resilient Shorten would be on the campaign trail. He was no Mark Latham, prone to derailing when the pressure was on.

State differences would also be crucial. Swings are never uniform, in the sense that the national results rarely allow an easy read across the pendulum to ascertain which sitting MPs would survive a swing against the government. Indeed, differences within states from electorate to electorate can also be significant. For example, in New South Wales Craig Laundy secured a swing to him in the seat of Reid, yet the swing against the government in Paterson where there was a retiring member reached double digits.

There are always stronger and weaker states for each major party, dictated by factors such as where the leader is more or less appealing, where the opposition leader hails from, how cashed up and organised particular state organisations are, and the state political issues that may be impacting on the federal campaign. The Country Fire Authority dispute in Victoria removed the otherwise traditional advantage Shorten might have expected in his home state. Equally, Turnbull's inability to appeal to Sydney's west, alongside the Medicare scare campaign, removed his home-state advantage. In the end New South Wales was the worst state for the Coalition in terms of seat losses. Victoria was the only state in which Labor lost a seat to the government.

Labor was hopeful of a strong showing in Queensland, with at least half a dozen government seats up for grabs. Labor claimed there was major movement in seats such as Brisbane, Bonner, Forde, Dawson and Capricornia. The government claimed that its track polling suggested it was holding the line in most of these seats. It didn't lose any of them. If it had, Turnbull would have lost his majority. Clive Palmer's decision to abandon his seat of Fairfax ensured the Coalition would add to their tally. Julie Bishop spent more time in Queensland than Turnbull, with her popularity in the sunshine state higher than the prime minister's, according to internal party research. Barnaby Joyce also headed north frequently, despite his showdown with Tony Windsor in New England. The importance of Queensland was confirmed when both leaders went to Brisbane in the first days of the campaign, with Shorten flying on to North Queensland, where the popular Liberal MP Ewen Jones was under threat in Herbert, centred on Townsville, which was about to become the object of a bidding war between the major parties. It was in regional Queensland that concerns about Turnbull's city-centric agenda of managing a transition from a mining-based economy to an innovation-driven economy caused the most angst. In the end Queensland largely held together for the conservatives, after long and drawn-out postal-vote counting.

South Australia presented a risky proposition for both major parties, with the Nick Xenophon Team capable of winning seats where its primary support eclipsed that of the second-placed major party candidate and received a strong flow of preferences all the way to victory. The state was 'harder to pick than a broken nose', as one Labor MP put it. The NXT factor turned notionally safe seats into three-cornered contests, meaning that anything could happen. NXT won Mayo and nearly picked up Grey.

Xenophon had long led the charge against the loss of manufacturing jobs in South Australia. He also received more credit than Labor for the government's decision to build next-generation submarines in Adelaide. While Liberal seats were under the most threat from NXT, Labor's vote suffered the most from the popularity of the media-savvy Xenophon. This would also have consequences in the Senate. Both major parties had to direct resources away from the marginal seats and hope that the unknown NXT candidates would ensure that voters would baulk at putting number one next to a name other than Xenophon. They found, though, that the psychology of such voters was like that of the Americans voting for Donald Trump; it was first and foremost a vote against being taken for granted by successive governments. Unmasking candidates as having shared a platform with extremists or as being anti-vaccination nuts was immaterial.

Throughout 2014, the Abbott government had backed away from its 2013 election pledge to build twelve new-generation submarines, in part to build a closer security relationship with Japan by purchasing Japanese submarines 'off the shelf'. Senator Sean Edwards took advantage of the first spill motion in early 2015 to promise Abbott the support of a handful of South Australian Liberals in return for a turnaround on the submarine issue.[5] The reversal was far from elegant, with Defence Minister Kevin Andrews announcing a hastily devised beauty contest that he called a 'comprehensive evaluation process'. With Labor and Xenophon adamant that the submarines be built locally, the policy emphasis shifted from saving Abbott's hide to saving the seats of Hindmarsh, Sturt and Boothby in the suburbs of Adelaide, as well as Jamie Briggs's seat of Mayo in the Adelaide Hills. There was no 'Whyalla wipeout' as a result of carbon pricing, but the steelworks came under threat when its parent company was placed into administration. The Commonwealth and state governments competed to suggest ways in which more Australian steel could be used in infrastructure projects. By building more infrastructure rather than talking about it would have been a good start.

There may have been a national security dimension to the decision to spend $50 billion on submarines, but that was far from clear to any observer of the political debate. Making the announcement that a French firm had won the contract, Turnbull enthused, 'this submarine program alone will see Australian workers build Australian submarines with Australian steel here where we stand today for decades into the future'. The free trader did his best Bob Katter impersonation. 'We do this to secure Australia, to secure our island nation,' he said. 'But we do it also to ensure that our economy transitions to the economy of the twenty-first century, that we have the technology and the skills and the advanced manufacturing and the jobs for our children and our grandchildren for decades to come.' This dimension of innovation policy put the pre-Christmas statement well and truly in the shade. The bower bird was prepared to pay handsomely for shiny submarines. No defence department estimate of the premium paid for building the submarines in Australia was released, but estimates based on other shipbuilding projects vary from 25 to 40 per cent, amounting to tens of billions of dollars. There aren't many sure things in electoral analysis. That the submarine decision was decisive, if rather expensive, in restoring the fortunes of the government in South Australia seemed assured.[6] Yet Edwards lost his Senate seat and the Liberals lost Hindmarsh.

Results in Western Australia often flow in a different direction to the rest of the country. The fiscal mismanagement of the state Liberal government had blunted the national message of the Coalition. Labor was hopeful it could win the new seat of Burt in the working class suburbs south-east of Perth, as well as seats that periodically change hands such as Cowan, Swan and Hasluck. It picked up Cowan, but not the other two Liberal-held electorates. A close election meant that the two-hour time difference between the east coast and Western Australia left a nervous wait for both parties on election night as the results rolled in.

Tasmania is a traditionally difficult state for the conservatives due to its high dependence on welfare spending. Abbott's strong performance in 2013 in winning the seats of Bass, Braddon and Lyons would be tough to repeat. Sweeping Tasmania, with the exception of independent Andrew Wilkie's seat of Denison, was essential to Labor forming government. For these reasons it is hard to know why Tasmania wasn't on the Coalition's radar, not that it's likely the government could have stemmed the bleeding from Mediscare in the nation's poorest state.

Both leaders were novices when it came to fronting federal elections. A long campaign ensured that their discipline would be tested, with more question marks over Turnbull than Shorten. The appearances of the leaders on the nightly news gave a misleading impression of the overall effort that goes into campaigns. They were the tip of the spear.

The Coalition's senior strategist, Mark Textor, believed Shorten was at risk of morphing into a figure like British former Labour leader Ed Miliband. Like Shorten, Miliband was confident that voters were tired of fiscal rectitude and market principles and would accept a left-wing alternative. While Miliband was performing strongly prior to the 2015 British campaign, the conservative government—advised by Textor and long-term collaborator Lynton Crosby—adopted a successful strategy of contrasting its steady economic management with the risks associated with a novice leader. This was the genesis of the idea that holding the Australian federal election shortly after the budget would leverage the advantage of incumbency to convince the electorate that the government had a plan for the future. Textor became frustrated by the lack of funds available to prosecute his strategy, and the Medicare scare campaign sucked the oxygen out of it in any event. While Turnbull would take responsibility for the result, the full leadership group signed off on the campaign strategy developed by Textor, federal director Tony Nutt, Turnbull and Sinodinos. Sinodinos would travel with Turnbull for most of the campaign, an indication of how dependent the prime minister had become on the former Howard confidant. Yet, Sinodinos's political judgement was no better than Turnbull's as it turned out. The group around Turnbull during the campaign had decades of experience but it's not clear they were providing him with the best advice.

The government's official campaign spokesman was the finance minister and special minister of state Senator Mathias Cormann. He was an Abbott supporter in the September leadership showdown, but the decision was made to stick with him as campaign spokesperson after the blemish-free job he had done in the same role in 2013. It was a decision driven by Tony Nutt and supported by Abbott's former deputy chief of staff, now Liberal HQ communications director Andrew Hirst. Not everyone agreed Cormann was the right person for the job, with sections of Turnbull's office arguing that they would be better off using a 'fresh face' such as new social-services minister Christian Porter. The decision was made to stick with Cormann because of his prodigious work ethic and knowledge of the budget particulars, and because as a senator he wouldn't need to fight to hold an electorate. Added to this, Porter as social-services minister risked being dogged by questions about his cuts to welfare on the campaign trail had he served as spokesman. Other contenders, such as Kelly O'Dwyer, also faced a challenge in their electorates. O'Dwyer's difficulties selling superannuation changes after the budget also precluded her from the role. As it turned out, Porter's seat went from safe to marginal at the election, superannuation magnified as an issue, and O'Dwyer's seat faced a more serious than anticipated challenge from the Greens.

The government hoped Cormann would leverage his knowledge as finance minister to keep the focus on the economy, rather than be drawn into a debate about which side of politics was better placed to oversee health and education. His opposite number was Senator Penny Wong, her third election in the role, sharing it this time with shadow finance minister Tony Burke in an effort to meet the government's economic message head-on. While they were disciplined performers, the official spokesperson had become an anachronism by 2016. It was suited to the days of highly controlled campaigns where a reliable voice could be pushed out to complement the role of the leaders. Wong's and Burke's sound performance on fiscal issues allowed Shorten a more wide-ranging brief but the election agenda would prove difficult to control due to digital media and the long campaign.

Both campaign managers had experience, with Labor's George Wright having overseen the 2013 federal election campaign and the new federal director of the Liberal Party, Tony Nutt, having held a range of state directorships over the years. Most recently he had been the NSW Liberal director for a state campaign that had run smoothly—although after the federal result critics did suggest the loss of seats in New South Wales were too numerous, given Mike Baird was a 'dream candidate'. While Nutt was known for his discipline, some within Liberal circles wondered whether he would embrace some of the newer elements of campaigning in a modern age. Those close to Nutt deny the accuracy of such criticisms, pointing to his long track record in campaigning, arguing that he has always sought to keep abreast of the latest techniques emerging from the United States and how they might be applied in the Australian context. Mark Textor defended Nutt's approach in the aftermath of the campaign, although it is hard to assess whether the defence was as much about preserving the pair's reputations as engaging with fair criticism. Use of social media and online advertising are areas Labor has been quicker to move into than the Coalition. Equally, there were concerns within Labor's ranks about Wright, whose experience was limited to a chaotic and losing campaign in 2013, but Rudd was widely blamed for that loss. Wright emerged from the 2016 campaign with his reputation enhanced, Nutt's damaged.

Sky News commenced its campaign coverage as soon as Turnbull announced his plans to prorogue parliament. It was in that atmosphere that Scott Morrison finalised his budget.

Budget 2016

Nobody could recall a budget so close to an election campaign. Scott Morrison's first budget would carry more political weight than most such documents. With almost every reform floating around the Treasury and policy think-tanks having been dismissed, what was left for the budget? There were usually good reasons for putting some distance between budget night and election day. Budget measures needed to be explained not only to the electorate but to backbenchers as well. More worryingly for Turnbull, Morrison was proving to be a poor salesman. He could be forgiven earlier in the year for struggling to keep up with Turnbull's changes of heart on tax policy, but he had yet to prove that he could successfully promote complex policy. There would be no hiding behind devices such as the 'on-water matters' that had kept journalists at bay when he was immigration minister. Morrison retreated behind slogans and attacks on the opposition in a portfolio where something better was required.

The centrepiece of the budget was an extension of corporate tax cuts beyond small- and medium-sized business to the largest companies. The full cost of the cuts would not be felt for ten years. This sparked a debate about the usefulness of budget projections. Given the problems that all recent governments have had with budget forecasting over one or two years, the whole idea of ten-year projections was bizarre. Labor took advantage of the growing envelope for budgeting by promising reductions in the budget deficit in the never-never of a ten-year projection. Turnbull at first denied that Treasury had costed individual budget measures that far into the future but days later Treasury Secretary John Fraser conceded to a Senate Estimates hearing that the ten-year figure was $48.2 billion. With some rounding, Labor had a $50-billion weapon for the campaign. This combined with a stream of reports that the major beneficiaries would be Australian banks and, because of a tax treaty with the United States, that country's treasury. Beyond this arcane discussion of budgeting, though, Turnbull had provided Shorten with the strongest possible contrast between their economic philosophies, and Shorten would prove effective at exploiting this when the two went head to head in election debates.

The main problem with the corporate tax cuts from a political perspective was that there wasn't much else in the campaign-eve budget either for voters or for kick-starting the economy. A tiny tax cut for middle-income earners was derided and barely mentioned during the campaign. Having spoken of the evils of bracket creep, whereby inflation pushes taxpayers into higher tax brackets without the need for governments to legislate higher taxes, Morrison insisted on this measure. Money to combat multinational tax avoidance didn't make up for earlier cuts to the Australian Taxation Office; incentives for internships were broadly welcomed except by trade unions; an extension of the popular instant asset write-off for small business would help the government campaign with its favourite constituency. Infrastructure spending was increased but, as was the case during Abbott's tenure as would-be infrastructure prime minister, was not keeping pace with declining spending by cash-strapped state governments.

As *The Sydney Morning Herald*'s Peter Hartcher pointed out, Turnbull was appealing to Australians as investors rather than workers.[7] In this sense Turnbull was making a similar mistake to John Howard's WorkChoices pitch. The Liberals have internalised the view of Australians as rugged individualists—future oriented and willing to take risks—when most are nervous about globalisation and see themselves as wage earners rather than potential entrepreneurs. Turnbull was particularly susceptible to this view of the electorate, which was only reinforced when his office wheeled him around to small businesses pre-screened to mouth the right words for the travelling media. Or, in a meet and greet that Turnbull's minders must have run through perfectly but was widely mocked on social media, showcasing a couple who were paying off a negatively geared property for their one-year-old daughter. The family's efforts may have been admirable but the episode only underlined Labor's questions about why other taxpayers should be subsidising such arrangements.

Much more attention was paid to the detail of the foreshadowed changes to superannuation. Winding back the generous concessions provided by Peter Costello when he was swimming in temporary mining revenue a decade earlier was widely expected. Labor had provided Turnbull with political cover by announcing its proposals a year earlier. The biggest problem with the superannuation changes was the perception of retrospectivity—particularly offensive to Liberal Party supporters protecting their nest eggs. This had some effect on the willingness of Coalition supporters to donate to local campaigns, and may have lost the parties some primary votes that would inevitably come back in preferences. More problematic was that the noisy campaign against the changes caused more voters to assume that they would be affected than was in fact the case. The proximity of the budget to the campaign caused problems when government figures, including deputy Liberal leader Julie Bishop, weren't across the detail in media interviews.

According to Essential Report, 37 per cent of voters thought the Coalition was more likely to reduce the deficit compared to 14 per cent who nominated Labor. Even Labor supporters don't know their own party's respectable fiscal record. This kind of ingrained belief gives Coalition governments more scope to overspend. In spite of the government's rhetoric on the deficit, the 2016 budget projected government spending as a proportion of the economy to increase until 2019–20—smaller government was always just around the corner.

The difference between the two deficit figures was trivial, given the margin of Treasury's forecasting errors over the past twenty years. The actual figure four years into the future would more than likely be some order of magnitude higher (or lower) than the difference between the parties. During the election campaign, though, the most important difference between the parties was the public trust deficit on budget matters.

The government sought an election about economic management, claiming only it could secure the country's fiscal future. Labor argued that its policy decisions offered long-term savings to the budget alongside necessary short-term spending on health and education. Newspoll showed the Coalition as the preferred economic managers, and this was expected to become the dominant theme by the end of the long campaign. However, the last Newspoll before the election was called was notable for Turnbull's net approval rating having fallen 50 percentage points from plus 38 to minus 12 since the first couple of months after he assumed the leadership.

'A plan for jobs and growth' was to be the campaign slogan for Turnbull's Coalition: a surfeit of nouns in contrast to Abbott's slogans full of 'real action'. Taking a more sophisticated approach to politics than Abbott wasn't a high bar. But what did 'jobs and growth' mean to the average voter? The risk for Turnbull was that calling an election slightly early, with a long eight-week campaign, which he had flagged two weeks earlier, could become the longest suicide note in political history. The hope that Turnbull's popularity would help him overcome Shorten butted heads with

Shorten's proven campaigning skills as a union leader. Then there were the two campaign units—Textor's proven strategists, Labor as a unit of proven grassroots organisers. This contest would be closer than most people expected, and certainly closer than Turnbull anticipated. The government entered the formal campaign period confident, but about to spend eight weeks fighting for an economic plan that sections of his own party were disillusioned about, with limited resources and all the while facing opponents who were battle-hardened for exactly this sort of campaign. Privately Turnbull worried that he had missed his window to win an easy election victory by going to the polls early, as Kevin Rudd had also failed to do at the end of 2009. Turnbull also wondered whether he'd have been better off to stick to his instincts and opt for a shorter campaign and a longer period in government, by lasting a full term. But it was too late. The plan was set and the trigger was informally announced two weeks before Turnbull visited the governor-general. There was no going back.

Six

EIGHT WEEKS IS A LONG TIME IN POLITICS

IT'S HARD TO recall an election campaign that hasn't been dubbed by its participants a 'historic choice'. While the length of the 2016 event made for some dull moments, there was still a lot at stake. It was a pity, then, that Isentia reported less interest in the 2016 campaign on talkback radio and social media than the 2013 contest. The major parties had lost the trust of voters just as they were providing a genuine choice for them. Since the failure of the Coalition's Fightback! package in 1993, opposition parties have favoured small-target strategies. The failure of Tony Abbott and Joe Hockey's 2014 budget, and the debate over fairness that it sparked, gave Bill Shorten confidence to differentiate Labor from the government in stronger terms. Shorten's boldness should have provided Turnbull with a target-rich environment. However, during and after the campaign there were questions about the Coalition's strategy of presenting Turnbull in a positive light.

The opposition was more honest about raising taxes in order to spend more on services. In contrast, the government argued that cuts to company taxes would spur growth, claiming a strong economy was the best way to fund social services. Shorten had spent the previous three years sharpening the differences between the parties on economic policy. He had flatly opposed changes to funding in health, education and pensions, and the deregulation of university fees in the 2014 budget. He forced the Coalition to play catch-up on winding back superannuation tax concessions, took a risk by rejecting negative gearing, and criticised Turnbull's proposed company tax cuts. Shorten had been the boldest leader of the opposition in decades, something he never failed to remind journalists of in his weekly ring-around. Of course, there were more successful opposition leaders than John Hewson to emulate. In the midst of these contrasts, the two parties sought to manufacture differences where there were none, in areas such as immigration and health.

The power of incumbency isn't what it once was, but the maths doesn't lie. Governments almost always win the close elections, especially at the federal level. Labor's challenge in attempting to win enough seats from the Coalition was compounded by the perception that the Greens would take at least one additional inner-city seat. Former party machine man David Feeney was defending the historically safe Melbourne seat of Batman, but revelations of his failure to declare a house in the electorate were followed by his inability to recall whether or not it was negatively geared, even though the tax issue had a high profile in the weeks before and after the budget. Usually a reliable Labor spokesman, Feeney did himself further harm with an absent-minded performance in his regular spot on Sky News. Labor also had to disendorse its candidate for Fremantle because of undisclosed criminal convictions, giving the Greens hope in the seat whose state namesake they once held. Anthony Albanese should have been a major asset in the national campaign but had to spend more time than he would have liked in his inner Sydney seat of Grayndler, where Labor's position on refugees was opposed vigorously by the Greens. Albanese had voted against boat turn-backs at Labor's national conference in 2015 but had to defend the official policy. He had the support of the otherwise conservative-leaning *Daily Telegraph*, which used a front page to promote its 'Save Albo' campaign. While Albanese won his seat comfortably in the end, resources had to be diverted from marginal contests against the government. The Liberals played their usual games about whether they would send preferences to the Greens before Labor, adding to the nervousness about these seats. The risk the Greens pose for Labor isn't merely electoral. The first week of the 2016 campaign saw an outbreak of dissent in Labor ranks over the party's asylum-seeker policies. Labor MPs expressing concerns on this front hailed from the left of the party, or were fighting three-cornered contests that included the Greens, or both.

Pandering to potential Greens voters was viewed by Labor strategists as political poison in outer metropolitan marginal seats, handicapping them in areas where Turnbull's polished prime-ministerial persona was less electorally enticing than Shorten's more earthy image. Shorten—having backed Julia Gillard's challenge to Kevin Rudd and therefore being at the epicentre of negotiations with the Greens and other crossbenchers in 2010 to avoid the ignominy of defeat after just one term—was forced to deny that he would form an alliance with the Greens after the election, no matter what. He was echoing Gillard's words ahead of the 2010 election as well as former Tasmanian Labor premier David Bartlett's ahead of his state election the same year. Greens campaign spokesperson Nick McKim recalled Bartlett describing him as the sum of all evil ahead of the 2010 polling day, only to do a deal to put the then Tasmanian Greens leader in the ministry as part of a Labor–Greens coalition immediately afterwards.

McKim said the pre-poll positioning of Labor would not match its post-poll negotiating position if a hung parliament demanded negotiations. The same would go for the Liberal Party. What Labor was ruling out, though, and what Turnbull was trying to exploit, was a formal deal such as Gillard had made with the crossbenchers. Gillard had thought that a deal that could apply in both houses put her in a strong position, but in the public mind the deal forced her to break election promises. With the polls remaining tight, Turnbull would soon be warning voters of the possibility of a return to minority government. In an era of professional political practice, incumbency—not ideological virtue—is the only currency that matters. The Coalition would happily ally itself with the Greens if doing so delivered it government, but the same couldn't be said about the Greens. For them ideological purity and political positioning go together. With nearly 90 per cent of Greens voters preferencing Labor ahead of the Liberals, shunning a governing alliance with the conservatives was not a difficult position to take. With the notable exceptions of fuel excise and the deal to reform the Senate voting system, the Greens had been loath to even deal with the conservatives. New leader Richard Di Natale slightly reconfigured this, but the loss of all the Australian Democrats senators over a decade, after the parliamentary party defied its membership to compromise with the Howard government on the GST following the 1998 election campaign, looms large for all minor parties. This picture may one day be complicated by the Greens making progress in wealthy inner suburbs of Sydney and Melbourne. State election results have underlined this possibility. The Greens promoted polling showing that they were competitive in Assistant Treasurer Kelly O'Dwyer's seat of Higgins but Liberal research never showed the seat under threat.

After Labor had been belted around by business interests on the mining tax and carbon pricing, little in their platform could be considered radical. These two Rudd- and Gillard-era taxes had been poorly presented despite the advantages of incumbency. The mining tax was unveiled too far into Labor's first term with little preparation, and carbon pricing was mishandled in any number of ways. Shorten was not going to be accused of springing economic policy on the electorate. The main contours of his strategy were clear prior to the campaign: some promises on elusive taxation of multinational corporations, tweaks to capital gains tax and negative gearing that had long been publicly debated, and the long-established changes to superannuation concessions. Labor matched the Coalition tax cut for small business but not the cuts for larger companies. Previous Labor victories from opposition had been accompanied by at least some support from a business community disillusioned with the

Liberal Party. Missing from Labor's formula this time around was any sense of how it would encourage business investment in the short term. Education funding was promoted as good for productivity but the benefits were projected decades into the future. Pro-investment policies would hardly have been inconsistent with an attack on Turnbull for being out of touch, given Labor's record on health and education. Shorten summarised this approach in his campaign launch:

> In the end, the choice for Australians is simple. If you want better schools, not richer banks—vote Labor. If you want a tax cut for local jobs, not a tax break for foreign shareholders—vote Labor. If you want a housing affordability plan that's more than—'get rich parents'—vote Labor. If you want a first-rate NBN for a first-rate economy—vote Labor.

Shorten's strategy left the opposition open to attacks—overegged in some quarters—of class warfare.[1] Treasurer Scott Morrison accused Shorten of declaring war on business. As he would on a number of occasions during the campaign, Turnbull let his ministers set the tone of government rhetoric. The prime minister could either embarrass his team or join them, so he joined Morrison's attack. 'He is declaring war on business,' Turnbull said of Shorten. 'He's taking a thoroughly anti-business approach and that can only lead to slower economic growth, a weaker economy, weaker revenues for the government, tax revenues for the government and less money to spend on schools and hospitals.' Unfortunately the war metaphor was carried too far when Morrison accused Labor of using 'tax as their bullets' at the very time that the bodies of thirty-three fallen Australian soldiers and their families were being repatriated from Malaysia. Neither Turnbull nor Shorten attended the ceremony in another sign of poor judgement from Turnbull's office.

These kinds of errors in the government's campaign were surprising, given the amount of coordination among the parliamentary leadership and between the parliamentary and organisational teams.

Poor relations between a leader's entourage and a party's organisational strategists have been blamed for many failed campaigns. Coalition tactics were confirmed during a daily telephone hookup at 6 a.m. featuring Turnbull, Sinodinos, Mark Textor and Tony Nutt. This was followed at 6.30 by a briefing for the wider leadership group. They also had a plan for dealing with the major media commentators. Prior to the campaign, the shock-jock Alan Jones, an Abbott supporter but not a delcon, could be won over. Delcon Andrew Bolt was to be ignored. Turnbull had worked on his relationship with *The Australian*'s new editor-in-chief, Paul 'Boris' Whitaker. Abbott had criticised that newspaper for not supporting the difficult reforms of his government vigorously enough under the previous editor. Whitaker was no fan of Turnbull, but emphasising the anti-business nature of Labor's policies would keep the likes of Whitaker on side. Turnbull would allow few high-profile interviews, even declining those with the talkback jocks so beloved of John Howard and Tony Abbott. The National Party had more licence to tailor the campaign for their own purposes than Liberal MPs—longstanding practice, given their different constituencies. The risk for Turnbull was that Nationals could use a long campaign to contradict their leader and the messaging Liberal strategists believed was their pathway to victory. Internal dissent within the conservative Coalition is always a recipe for campaign dysfunction.

Sky News was as keen to host the campaign leaders' debates as the free-to-air commercial networks were keen to eschew their responsibility to properly cover such national events. The first leaders' debate was styled as a 'people's forum', a format Sky had run over a few campaign cycles where a club in the suburbs of one of the capital cities—in this case in the electorate of Macquarie in western Sydney—stands in for middle Australia. Undecided voters chosen by a polling company ask questions of the leaders. This format proved to be much more interesting than the traditional debate format in 2013 since both Kevin Rudd and Tony Abbott fancied their chances of empathising with voters. As we have seen, however, empathy is not Turnbull's strong suit. Sometimes he doesn't even try to fake it. Questions with factually incorrect premises showed what a tough job political persuasion can be. It's hard to start a conversation with an undecided voter by telling them they are wrong.

Unnervingly for Turnbull, the questions from the floor were not what he was used to from the press gallery. The voters weren't interested in generalisations like 'jobs and growth'. Their concerns were about either more specific policy detail or off the main issues of the campaign altogether. Shorten was much more skilled than Turnbull at bringing the debate back to his familiar themes without being seen to ignore the substance of the questions. This exchange captures Turnbull's inept performance:

> TURNBULL: As I said, in fact at Westpac's 199th birthday recently—I gave the banks a—Westpac and the other bankers there a bit of a—a lecture.
>
> SHORTEN: I believe it is well overdue to have a royal commission into Australia's banks.
>
> TURNBULL: He said, 'Time to put the banks in the dock,' as though they're accused of a crime, as though they're all criminals. (Applause from audience member.) Now I believe—I believe—well, let me just say—let me just say to you.
>
> SHORTEN: I'm not saying banks are criminals, but what I am saying is ...
>
> TURNBULL: Well why would they go in the dock?
>
> (Laughs from audience)
>
> Why would you put them in the dock?

SHORTEN: Oh, I bet they just went home and changed their—changed their practices after a lecture from you.

(Laughs from audience)

Laughing at the prime minister. Not a good look. While not many Friday-night television viewers chose the debate over the football, this exchange was widely reported in the rest of the media. As was the fact that Turnbull had a poor debate—wanting to catch his opponent out more so than communicate with voters about their concerns.

Perhaps most importantly, the debate exposed the 'plan for jobs and growth' as thin gruel. The Liberals' own publications underlined this problem. The 'strong new economy' the Coalition promoted was headlined by the science and innovation package launched by Turnbull in December 2015—fine on its merits but modest and unlikely to appeal to the majority of workers in traditional forms of employment. They were more concerned about keeping their present job and getting a wage rise than where the next generation of jobs would come from. Next was the Defence Industry Plan, targeted to a handful of seats and again outside the experience of the majority. Tax cuts were next. It wouldn't be a Coalition campaign without them. Turnbull was weak, though, on linking tax cuts to growth in a way that would help him as he engaged with voters—at least when he wasn't standing in one of the small businesses that would benefit directly. It wasn't clear how the average voter would benefit from giving cuts to big business. Worse, Turnbull defended the $50-billion price tag by pointing out that the most expensive cuts didn't even begin during the next parliament, and so weren't going to turbo-charge the economy any time soon.

Spending on health, education and roads was also mentioned in the plan, but this was mostly defensive. Voters overwhelmingly supported Labor's position on the first two. Restoring the rule of law was thrown in so Turnbull could claim that the Australian Building and Construction Commission double-dissolution trigger was worth the effort. The document also recycled the canard of promising job growth that seemed impressive—'more than 200,000' in this case—but was about the rate Treasury had been forecasting anyway. Incumbent prime ministers can make a positive case about a modest set of proposals—belt tightening, an uncertain global outlook etc. Turnbull's problem was that he was promoting himself to the public as Liberal leader for the first time, and while this collection of shiny objects said something about the bower bird, there wasn't much to connect him in any meaningful way to the electorate.

Turnbull did better in the second debate on ABC television but it was a staid affair. Questioning from journalists was arguably a much sharper test of the policy positions of the leaders but they were also more predictable, and the traditional debate format allowed the leaders to fall back on mini speeches. Shorten was just as flat in this format, where his empathy with voters was less of an advantage. In a worrying sign for the ability of Australia's political class to keep the electorate engaged, only half a million viewers tuned in. While more than the first debate, where ABC News 24 was the only terrestrial channel to pick up the Sky News feed, only a fifth of that small audience persevered through the full tedious hour.

A long campaign with relatively few high-profile policy announcements gave observers plenty of time to analyse every utterance of the deposed prime minister and his chief of staff. Former Howard staffer Paula Matthewson labelled Abbott and Credlin's strategy a good cop–bad cop routine, with Abbott arguing for a return of the Turnbull government while Credlin needled the prime minister. It may simply have been the case that Credlin was motivated to criticise Turnbull quite independently of how Abbott was feeling. She lost as much as he did when the coup succeeded. She criticised 'Mister Harbourside Mansion' for skipping a planned street walk in the seat of Lindsay. Yet her appearances on Sky News and columns in the News Corp Sunday papers were pretty tame—especially compared to what she was getting up to behind the scenes, using her old trick of backgrounding journalists.

Credlin had long been close to many journalists; it was one of the sticky points in her role as chief of staff to Abbott that she was in such close contact with the Fourth Estate. Once out of the staffing game Credlin was free to pursue her own interests, and after the criticisms she had copped during her time working for Abbott few could begrudge her the opportunity to leverage her profile to offer comment on how the new PM—someone she was convinced had spent two years undermining Abbott's prime ministership—was faring.

Tensions between Morrison and Turnbull were an early target of Credlin's attention. She pointed out to journalists privately that Morrison had been 'taken out of the freezer' when he started doing a little more media earlier on in the campaign. While Morrison had been regularly appearing in front of the cameras, it was true that he wasn't cutting through. Credlin made the valid point that 'he's supposed to be one of the heavy hitters in any government. If he's not [cutting through] then you've got to start to get worried.' Morrison's positioning as a natural conservative successor to Abbott who had switched to the Turnbull camp made him an easy target. Credlin took the view that 'The current PM and treasurer don't trust each other', a point she was keen to ensure colleagues in the media were aware of. She was especially scathing of the costings stunt Cormann and Morrison attempted to pull early in the campaign. The claims about Labor's foreign-aid spending were the target of Credlin's criticism. 'How they got it so wrong is either internal CHQ [campaign headquarters] incompetency (someone missed picking up the Plibersek revision to their foreign aid spend) or it was taken out by CHQ and then overruled by a minister to put it back in. Whatever the real reason it has distracted from an attack that should have been much stronger for the government,' Credlin texted colleagues. She was probably right, adding: 'You don't get many chances to throw a costings bomb and this one didn't even make the front of the news packages.'

Credlin was particularly scathing of the PM not attending the Sydney repatriation ceremony for Vietnam soldiers. She pointed out to colleagues informally at Sky that Abbott had regularly attended similar events, and it was inappropriate for Turnbull not to do the same, especially as he was in Sydney on the day of the ceremony. Credlin told her colleagues to look into whether Abbott had even been invited. We can confirm that Abbott had contacted colleagues himself to express his anger at not having been invited. It is impossible to know if the Credlin–Abbott criticisms were coordinated, but at the very least they were of the same mind on this issue.

Nobody should underestimate the extent to which Credlin was backgrounding a host of journalists about when, how and why Turnbull was making errors on the campaign. As a new member of the Fourth Estate she provided useful help for colleagues, using her extensive knowledge as an insider to fill out criticisms that otherwise might not have been as powerfully delivered. News of such criticisms seeped back to the Prime Minister's Office and Turnbull himself. Pamela Williams reported that Turnbull's office told Sky that Turnbull would not appear on any more debates on the network as long as Credlin was a commentator there.[2] There would be no more debates. Shorten mocked Turnbull over this decision—'I've sought him here. I've sought him there ...'—but a bit of mockery was tolerable compared to another platform that gave the leaders equal billing.

Meanwhile, a Supreme Court decision in Papua New Guinea just prior to the campaign threatened to bring the refugee issue back front and centre. While the closure of the Manus Island detention centre was a challenge for the government, it gave the immigration minister Peter Dutton the excuse he needed to remind voters that returning Labor to power would see the flow of boat arrivals resume. Dutton put asylum-seekers back on the agenda in the second week. Paul Murray teed up the issue on Sky by asking Dutton about the Greens policy of raising the refugee intake to 50,000. Off he went. 'They won't be numerate or literate in their own language, let alone English,' he claimed. 'These people would be taking Australian jobs, there's no question about that. For many of them that would be unemployed, they would languish in unemployment queues and on Medicare and the rest of it so there would be huge cost and there's no sense in sugar-coating that, that's the scenario.' Whatever your prejudice against refugees, Dutton had you covered. The interview had been cleared with Turnbull's office but not the detail of Dutton's comments, which saw him freelancing. The problem was that the jobs claim applied equally to the broader migration program. Nevertheless, Turnbull backed his minister.

Media Strategy

Not so long ago, a day in the life of an election campaign consisted of the two major-party leaders arranging their mornings around images for the nightly broadcast television news—a shopping-centre walk or a childcare centre—and perhaps an evening interview or fundraiser. Not much else happened so the right messages dominated the media cycle. Digital media has transformed that cycle, not so much for the leaders but because the amount of media space has so dramatically expanded there is a greater role for other senior figures and local candidates. There is always a handful of candidates (and a few frontbenchers) who need to be hidden away for the duration of the campaign, but leaving spaces such as Sky News and social media open to opponents and hostile interest groups is risky.

It's a long time since election advertising in Australia demanded that the best minds in the business come up with memorable pitches such as Gough Whitlam's 'It's Time' jingle. Campaign advertising is now brief, simple and to the point. Leaders' faces, looking authoritative or sinister depending on who is paying, bold graphics, no music. The main virtue, other than the low cost, is the versatility. With little investment in the cost of producing the spot, it can be quickly dropped to any media outlet interested in spruiking what's 'new' in the campaign advertising space. It may not even run in a paid placement as long as it gets attention courtesy of the media running the web version. There was nothing exciting about Turnbull's pitch. The Coalition did try something different—a tradesman complaining about negative gearing and, rather dubiously, the notion of a banking inquiry. The tagline, no doubt taken directly from a focus group, was the uninspiring 'let's stick with the current mob for a while'. Ridicule was the primary response. This was a good example of mainstream media picking up sentiment from social media and feeding it back into the campaign. The difficult thing to observe is the extent to which any of this kind of commentary reaches the target audience for the ad or whether the ad itself was effective because it was inserted into programming watched by swinging voters.

Labor had been running aggressive ads since the beginning of the campaign, attacking Turnbull personally as well as alleging that the Coalition planned to cut services. Critics questioned whether the deluge would lose its potency come polling day.

While voices in favour of a sharper Coalition campaign against Shorten were heard via the media, backbenchers were also making this point to campaign headquarters, along with criticism of the repetitive main slogans. Strategists such as Textor can be contemptuous of this kind of criticism. He stuck to the axiom that only insiders were sick to death of hearing 'jobs and growth'. The Coalition campaign justified its relatively positive advertising pitch on the grounds that it would shift to strong attack ads in the final weeks, following through until the electronic advertising blackout in the final days, as well as in the newspapers thereafter. The strategy was for early messages that were deliberately non-confrontational in order to 'bait' swinging voters before 'switching' their vote to the Coalition in the final week. Marketing gurus often cite the 'bait and switch' approach to commercial advertising. The risk for the Coalition was that if its bait and switch strategy was left too late, Labor's attack ads may have already cruelled Turnbull's image beyond repair. Equally, if negative ads attacking Shorten were left too late he might already appear as a viable alternative PM, making cutting him down harder. Liberal strategists argued that most campaigns are only four or five weeks long, and parties rarely ramp up their attack ads ahead of the final fortnight. The risks were that unexpected events, candidate mistakes and leaders getting themselves into trouble during otherwise highly controlled media appearances could derail the most well-orchestrated strategy. These were the unknowns that no amount of planning could avoid.

The major party campaigns had two separate yet intertwined elements to them: the free media the leaders generated, as Shorten and Turnbull traversed the continent spruiking their messages, and the targeted professional campaigns emanating from the major party campaign headquarters (CHQ). The latter included a large media unit, to engage with the journalists both following the leaders and based out of Canberra. There was also a social-media contingent, responsible for keeping local candidates up to date with the latest happenings, including breaking news that might impact on the party's political responses. Daily talking points were distributed to all candidates, updated by SMS throughout the day. Secure websites provided shell pamphlets and other paraphernalia that could be tailored to suit individual electoral contests. The most important component to the CHQ operations was the coordinating of the paid advertising and the research that helped target resources at key marginal seats. This was the macro effort to use advertising at the nationwide level, alongside the micro seat-by-seat operations essential to winning enough seats to govern.

The battle for free media reporting—rather than paid advertising—saw two very different approaches by the major party leaders in 2016. Labor tried to keep Shorten busy, using as many opportunities as presented themselves to elevate his standing as the alternative prime minister and to boost his name recognition among an often politically disengaged public. He was free and available for whatever opportunity existed to square off against the PM: debates, people's forums, even a Facebook showdown. Immediately after the Facebook debate Shorten was out publicly calling for another debate. The Shorten campaign didn't limit itself to one media event per day, and if daily events unexpectedly developed, a rapid response often occurred—via a media appearance, a policy adjustment or even a social-media post. It contrasted starkly with the Turnbull strategy—a more traditional one event per day, fewer questions at media conferences and a more secretive itinerary. Journalists who swapped between the two camps reported that Team Turnbull was more tightly controlled, less engaged in the debates of the day, and clearly more interested in minimising errors than maximising opportunities. Turnbull's was the strategy of a frontrunner, confirmed by polling in marginal seats even when the national two-party vote was close. Team Turnbull, some journalists thought, 'treats us like mushrooms'. The government relied on its paid advertising strategy and capacity to sandbag seats, although the media blackout in the final days of the campaign limited the effectiveness of this strategy just when it needed to rebut Shorten's Medicare attack.

One of the reasons why the campaign wasn't reporter-friendly was that both sides already had a lot of policy on the record. Budgets usually provide months of new stories as the detail seeps into the community. While some of that detail emerged at unfortunate times during the Coalition's election campaign, the budget itself receded quickly from view. Existing policy isn't news even if understanding the detail may have been important to voters during the campaign.

The cost of all this was paid in part by Turnbull reaching into his own pocket, reportedly finding a million dollars in spare change. This was widely derided by a media that shows almost zero interest in the issue of political donations. Voters should be much more worried about a donation of half that size from a corporation or union. Big business, much better at lobbying than campaigning, provided its usual useless contribution—lecturing the rest of Australians about the need for yet more economic reform. The only less welcome third-party endorsement came from real-estate agents supporting the Coalition's position on negative gearing—indicating who really benefits from that taxpayer subsidy. Turnbull had been in the past an advocate of reform of political funding. Perhaps he found his own way to limit the effects of outside groups.

Coalition HQ was happy with the first half of the campaign. Avoiding big spending commitments helped the Coalition dominate the local media cycle. Announcements of small initiatives in marginal seats helped with good headlines in a long campaign. Of course, this comes at the cost of involving the Commonwealth in matters best dealt with by state and local government, such as security cameras and sporting infrastructure. It is an important part of the campaign that no single journalist or political operative can really assess prior to counting the votes, especially in the modern era of multiple platforms and outlets.

The Only Thing to Fear ...

Franklin Delano Roosevelt's 1933 advice that the only thing we have to fear is fear itself could be applied in Australia ahead of the 2016 election: to voters, the opposition and the government. There was little need to fear Labor's ETS plans, for example, since the lion's share of work to reduce emissions wouldn't even commence until the mid-2020s, exposing Labor's claimed emissions-reduction targets as mere posturing. This was a sign that the strategists within the opposition had made a two-fold decision: they didn't want to damage their left flank by shunning climate-change action, but they feared a scare campaign against them if they outlined short-term binding targets to show how they would reach their long-term goal. Delcons such as Rowan Dean imagined Abbott destroying Labor on the basis of attacks on carbon trading or negative gearing. The government preferred to focus on the totality of Labor's supposedly anti-business platform in contrast with their plan for ... well, you know.

Fear was the government's biggest internal problem because it risked marginal-seat holders publicly distancing themselves from the overall strategy, giving rise to an ill-disciplined campaign that would jeopardise seats. Whenever the polls showed the Coalition falling marginally behind Labor, backbenchers' fear of losing their jobs would provide journalists with plenty of anonymous commentary on Mark Textor's strategy. Turnbull's personal approval continued to weaken before and even during the campaign, and while Shorten was not faring any better on that front, he was drawing closer as preferred prime minister. Coalition and Labor strategists alike knew that these numbers weren't necessarily indicators of voting intentions, just disappointment in Turnbull. Any complacency was knocked out of Turnbull's camp; the danger was that it would be replaced by the same panic among nervous backbenchers that had benefited him throughout 2015.

Scholarship on elections has long supported the view that negative campaigning is more effective than positive messaging. However, negative campaigning also has more substance than positive campaigning, which tends to centre on image and personality. Indeed, as political-marketing researcher Andrew Hughes has commented, one of the reasons why positive advertisements fail is that they often feature politicians trying to convince us of their sincerity, causing voters to tune out right away. While the government ran positive advertisements in the early weeks, portraying the Turnbull team in a positive light, it didn't take long for the overall tone of the campaign to turn negative. There was a lot of debate during and after the campaign about whether the Coalition went hard enough against Shorten. All sitting MPs were instructed by CHQ to make their first mailout of the campaign a letter above Turnbull's signature outlining his plan for jobs and growth. Some were not thrilled with this tactic but complied nevertheless. The positive tone would have been more suited to an early election that took advantage of the new leader's popularity. Instead, the Coalition strategy was attempting to take advantage of a leader whose approval rating was well off its peak. Turnbull's essential optimism would make a relentlessly negative election campaign too jarring. Labor's 'contrasts', as the Americans call attack ads, compared their plans for spending on health with the Coalition's alleged cuts, and investment in education with Turnbull's plans for a tax cut for business. Not that Labor's campaign shunned the embrace of fear as a political weapon: fear of big corporates not paying their fair share of tax (never mind that literally half of the electorate pay no net income tax); fear that the banks might be engaged in systemic fraud, hence the need for a royal commission into exactly what they were up to.

Attack ads against Shorten tested poorly with focus groups put together by the Coalition, while the exact opposite was true when

Labor tested negative attacks on Shorten with its focus groups in a bid to plan to counter Coalition attacks when they came. In the end few targeted negative attack ads were launched by the Coalition, but that didn't stop Turnbull attacking Shorten himself. Turnbull got better at the negative attacks after a couple of weeks—shrinking into the job of campaigner. One Labor spot that got the government's attention linked Labor's policy strengths in health and education to Turnbull's privileged background. The ad claimed that the fact he had never needed government help for these services meant that he took them for granted and couldn't be trusted to fund them properly. Liberal focus groups suggested that this message hit the mark with voters much more strongly than Turnbull's wealth or his business affairs. Yet it took a while for the Coalition campaign to respond with an ad featuring Turnbull talking about his father. Turnbull's message about the importance of his family was 'at once non-political and deeply political' and juxtaposed with images of Turnbull greeting families on his street walks.[3]

This focus on leaders was a crucial battle but a difficult one in which to change established voter perceptions. Many voters navigate the issue agenda of the campaign depending on how much they trust each leader to keep their promises in any given area. Voters either don't know the policy detail or doubt that it will be implemented. Building trust is especially difficult from opposition, but since John Howard's ascendancy the major parties have chosen repeatedly to throw away the chief advantage of incumbency—the known quantity, for good or ill—of the prime minister's character.

Midway through the campaign there was a curious consensus about the state of play. While published national polls showed either a dead heat or small Labor lead, polling in marginal seats confirmed the difficulty that Labor would have in winning more than a dozen additional seats. But of course published polls aren't what they once were, with automated messages replacing an actual pollster on the line, and the use of landlines instead of mobiles significantly limiting the reach of such polling. The media increasingly adopted the Coalition's rhetoric about the possibility of a minority

Labor government. This was, in the public's mind, something to be avoided, associated as it was with a revolving-door Labor leadership and the broken promise on carbon pricing. The fact that the 2010–13 hung parliament was as productive in terms of legislation as any recent cycle paled in significance compared with this negative image.

Both the major parties saw it as in their interests to release internal polling that indicated Labor was the underdog. Even then, it's likely that Labor was exaggerating its upside. Textor tried to keep Liberals from complacency. While it is hard to know what is spin and what is truly reflected in the research, the Coalition appeared genuinely confident that it could win somewhere between 79 and 83 seats, which is why most were surprised by the 76-seat result. Long campaigns have a varied track record as to whether they favour the government or the opposition. In 1984 Bob Hawke announced a long campaign and opposition leader Andrew Peacock manufactured a surprisingly good result, although the Labor government retained office. In 2004 John Howard used a long campaign to overcome Mark Latham's initial polling advantage, ultimately increasing the Coalition's majority. The Coalition was hoping Labor's negative-gearing policy would raise similar doubts for voters that Latham's Medicare Gold policy ultimately did in 2004 by the time the election rolled around. There was also a sense, though, that in spite of Turnbull's lethargic campaigning, the government was likely to prevail.

Seven
MEDISCARE

AT THE MID-POINT of the campaign, although Labor remained competitive in the published polls, there was a growing sense among commentators as well as inside the government that the incumbents would win. Turnbull was becoming more comfortable on the stump. The debates were behind him. Indeed, by the time of Labor's official launch, with three weeks left to polling day, its campaign appeared to be in the midst of a strategic retreat. Shorten's team had started to plan for another term in opposition, and how to ensure continuity of the leadership. The polls remained tight but difficult decisions were being made about how much money to spend on a doomed campaign. Winning individual seats was no longer a focus of the national campaign for Labor. Individual candidates would have to overcome the Coalition's sandbagging with their own resources. With the campaign in its final stretch, the choice for Labor was to spread resources too thin and risk winning a handful of seats or to shore up its primary vote to ensure a respectable result. It went for the latter. The difficulty, especially in the week of a campaign launch, was to avoid appearing as though the party had given up the goal of forming majority government. Hence the focus on Medicare, an issue that united swinging voters with Labor's heartland, but ultimately a defensive scare campaign. While anything can happen in the dying days of a campaign, when many swinging voters are still making up their minds, shifting the emphasis away from the economic issues that had defined Shorten's leadership would raise questions about Labor's tactics, which until this critical moment had appeared sound. Labor had always intended to pivot to Medicare but during the last week of the campaign, not the last three weeks. The Medicare attack was designed not just to appeal more to swinging voters (as well as galvanising Labor voters) but to show that Shorten was playing to win, even though Labor faced difficult choices about how to use its scarce campaign resources.

Shorten received some good news late in the campaign—Labor's track polling and focus-group research had picked up an unusually high concern with health funding. After further testing it was clear Labor had tapped into a rich vein of distrust voters had with the government—the trick would be exploiting it to maximum effect. This would become a matter for the professionals running the advertising, daily speaking notes and robo calls direct to households. But Shorten knew what the news meant—he had a pathway to victory, so he quickly contacted natural supporters in the media to alert them to the need not to lose hope. This election was winnable. Shorten's team knew the importance of keeping the dream alive, but they also knew doing so would help their boss retain the leadership in an honourable defeat.

In the final fortnight of a campaign the goal can change to one of 'saving the furniture' or, if things go better than expected, reaching out to seats not previously thought to be in play. We saw that in 2013, when resources on both sides of the partisan divide were increasingly deployed to safe Labor seats. These decisions were essential in 2016 because of the overall task Abbott's 2013 victory had left the opposition. When one party has a landslide win, there tends to be plenty of seats that the opposition can win back fairly easily at the following poll. This expectation was built into Shorten's task. If he conceded that victory was impossible and 10 seats would be a good fightback, he would maximise his chances of keeping the leadership. Such a result would bring Labor up to 65 seats, 11 short of a majority. For context, that would be the same disappointing result Beazley delivered in 2001 at the *Tampa* election. He resigned as leader the following day.

In a sign of how much time everyone had to spare during the long campaign, Labor sought partisan advantage in an area of bipartisanship—the misuse of entitlements by the major parties. Labor and the Liberals operate sophisticated software to track voters for the purpose of political communication.[1] The parties have exempted themselves from privacy laws to make the operation of these databases legal. Parliamentary entitlements are used to fund the software—with Labor charging its MPs directly before kicking some of that money the way of its software company Magenta Linas. The Liberal Party does it differently. Its company charges the MPs directly, then kicks back surplus monies to the Liberals. Unlike the company Labor uses (which also services trade unions), the Liberal company, Parakeelia, is wholly owned and operated by the Liberal Party. A simple survey of the finance department website shows the way Labor operates, and Shorten's own disclosures show his frequent claiming of the full 'software allowance' since entering parliament.

That such things were debated in the middle of the campaign showed that neither party was really ready for the long slog. If Labor left it too late to ramp up its charges against government health policy, the electorate may have already made up its mind. Too early and health would not be on the minds of late-deciding voters. The electorate had been primed for Labor's Medicare strategy by a number of doctors' groups. Just before the campaign the government struck a deal with Pathology Australia, which had collected hundreds of thousands of signatures in its campaign against changes to bulk-billing incentives. The Royal Australian College of General Practitioners funded a TV spot about the government's Medicare rebate freeze with a tagline that could have been written by Labor HQ: 'In Australia, your wealth should never affect your health.' There were petitions in offices and conspicuous signs foreshadowing fee increases and explaining why.

Scare campaigns on Medicare have been a Labor staple for decades—helped along by the ideological hostility of many in the Coalition to the socialised system. Since John Howard made peace with Medicare after the 1993 election, Coalition governments have tinkered around its edges, while keeping the essence of universal insurance. To be credible, scare campaigns need to have a modicum of truth to them. That was thought to be the problem with Bill Shorten's claim that the Coalition wanted to privatise Medicare. The claim made no sense, since Medicare is an inherent loss-maker and has always relied heavily on private provision of medical services, and Labor figures were on the record in favour of privatising the archaic payments system. Journalists, while falling short as they always do of accusing political leaders of lying, derided Shorten's formulation. However, with Medibank Private having been privatised within the current parliament, and privatisation generally being unpopular, the slogan did get the attention of voters, since the issue essentially came down to trust. Labor had earlier in the year mounted a successful scare campaign on the GST, with Shorten stalking every grocery shopper he could find to warn them about the price of lettuce if the GST was extended to fresh food. The approach reflected Labor focus-group research that showed voters were concerned about healthcare delivery under the Coalition, which had sought to legislate fiscal cuts to rein in recurrent expenditure on health and education. Government emphasis on improving the efficiency of these systems wasn't the stuff of inspirational campaigning.

The Coalition used its own scare campaigns on economic management and asylum-seeker boats to prise blue-collar workers away from Labor. And the Coalition was not about to win a truth-telling contest against the opposition. Turnbull continued Abbott's farcical tactic of referring to trade agreements as 'export agreements', as though the government had finally made mercantilism pay dividends hundreds of years after it was abandoned by the rest of the world. The reason for these word games is that while voters understand the importance of trade, and a majority expect trade agreements to benefit the economy, Essential Research has found that only a quarter of workers expect recent trade agreements to benefit them. Emphasising exports implicitly concedes that many workers in import-competing industries will lose their jobs. Perhaps more importantly, while it is understandable that an optimist like Turnbull would promote open trade and investment as prime minister, he needed to empathise more during the campaign with those whose jobs might be under threat in the here and now.

There was plenty of scope for Labor to attack the Coalition over health policy. The GP co-payment policy was a broken promise, and freezing the Medicare rebate for six long years was certain to put pressure on bulk-billing rates. Equally, effectively forcing fixed rents on GPs who house pathology services at their surgeries through payment structures was both unfair and illiberal. The health minister, Sussan Ley, had a low profile during the campaign, under orders from CHQ. Meanwhile, opposition health spokesperson Catherine King was prominent, seeking out GPs abandoning bulk-billing to embarrass the government. One obstacle to Labor's campaign was that bulk-billing rates were at an all-time high of over 80 per cent, as the government liked to point out. However, this was the figure for the total number of services billed, including the burgeoning number of tests and scans that are bulk billed. Bulk-billing for GP visits had indeed fallen since the rebate freeze, and the real stories of GPs changing their billing arrangements was much more effective in bringing the issues before voters than any statistics. It was understandable that Ley would have been kept out of the national media as the campaign began. To continue to keep her under wraps when Mediscare was unveiled, though, was a sign of the government's complacency.

Labor and supportive unions used robo calls to mislead voters about a privatisation agenda that didn't exist, with wild claims such as if you got cancer you were more likely to die if the Liberals retained government, because of their intention to privatise

Medicare. Even Ian Harper, who had overseen the bipartisan competition-policy review, slammed Labor for using a Productivity Commission recommendation on outsourcing Medicare services to claim the Liberals had a secret privatisation agenda. And the Australian Medical Association—which had been a big critic of the government's handling of health issues—condemned Labor for a false scare campaign on Medicare.

Health is an unusual policy area. Whatever its problems, single-payer socialised health is much more efficient than private insurance. Of course, when a government attempts to use its purchasing power to lower costs in areas where health providers are bilking taxpayers, the opposition screams blue murder. So it was when Sussan Ley announced changes to rebates for pathology and radiology. The government buckled in the early days of the 2016 campaign. It was on safer ground when it came to the freeze on Medicare rebates to GPs. The danger was that doctors would abandon bulk-billing and introduce their own co-payments. This blunted the Australian Medical Association's very public campaign against the government.

In the ultimate of ironies, in order to scuttle Labor's scare campaign Turnbull quashed any changes to outsourcing Medicare services, including the running of IT, for example. That (disappointingly) left the Coalition more committed to keeping every aspect of Medicare operations in public hands than Labor was. During that week Labor's Catherine King confirmed on ABC radio that Labor would consider outsourcing Medicare services if elected. There's no surprise in that, given the now shadow treasurer, Chris Bowen, got the ball rolling on just such a change in operations when he was human-services minister in the Rudd government in 2009.

Perhaps the most embarrassing public carping about what Liberals might do to Medicare came from former PM Bob Hawke. The one-time great Labor leader participated in a campaign advertisement for the first time since leaving office, warning that the Liberals were planning to privatise Medicare. The grand old man of Labor was used by Team Shorten, which clearly has as little regard for his honour as it does for the way he governed in the 1980s and '90s—the politics of envy and attacks on business that personified Labor's 2016 election campaign were shunned in the name of historic policy outcomes like the Prices and Incomes Accord when Hawke was PM.

But to complete the absurdity of Hawke fronting such an ad, one only has to delve ever so briefly into Hawke's policy track record on health. His leadership came undone at the hands of Paul Keating when Hawke, realising the fiscal pressures mounting on the health budget, sought to institute a Medicare co-payment.[2] Yes that's right, the very same policy Labor was now using to claim the Coalition would privatise Medicare if re-elected. The *Daily Telegraph* portrayed Shorten on its front page as Pinocchio. Judging by the swing towards Labor, Sydneysiders must have become inured to this sort of barracking from the city's biggest-selling newspaper, learning to flip straight to the sport pages.

The scare campaign over health was difficult to prosecute, though, given that Labor had joined the government in abandoning the large projections in hospital spending increases from the last Gillard–Swan budget of 2013. After years of accusing the government of responsibility for tens of billions of dollars in cuts when treasurer Joe Hockey announced changes to indexing in his first budget, during the campaign Shorten positioned the opposition just a couple of billion dollars ahead of the government's forecast spending on hospitals. The focus on Medicare was similar to some of Labor's rhetoric on business—playing well with the party faithful but not effective enough in winning marginal seats. In both cases, Labor needed swinging voters to share its distrust of the prime minister. This is why voter behaviour is more complicated than the campaign trinkets, like ABC's Vote Compass, suggest. Many of the voters who make their decision during the campaign have very limited information about party policies. They associate particular policies with each of the major parties and they make judgements about the trustworthiness of the leaders. Superior policies don't play a great role in this equation. Hence, the Coalition can blow out the budget deficit because voters trust it on economic policy. Labor can abandon Gillard's promises on health funding because the public expects Medicare to be safe in its hands.

Within days of Shorten's attack, posters began to appear stating, 'I guarantee Medicare stays,' over Turnbull's signature. The short television advertisements that had long been highlighting Turnbull's positive message on jobs and growth were edited to rebut the Medicare charge. An election campaign about not very much had suddenly become all about trust. John Howard had stunned the cynical press gallery when he framed the 2004 election around trust. 'Who do you trust to keep interest rates low' was his pitch. Whatever Howard's absolute levels of public trust after decades as a political warrior, he knew that he only needed voters to trust him more than an untested opposition leader—and it turns out Australia dodged a bullet in trusting Howard over Mark Latham. Shorten's role in the downfall of successive Labor prime ministers added to the usual public scepticism of opposition leaders. Turnbull had based his initial pitch around areas in which the public does trust Coalition stewardship—economic management. He was about to find out how much the public trusted him over health policy. In hindsight it is unclear what Turnbull could have done about Mediscare other than change the subject. Once again the long campaign made this difficult. Most policy had already been announced and the slow pace gave Labor time to hammer home its message.

The Labor claim that the Liberals would sell the entire service morphed into plans to privatise only parts of it, before dipping in the final days of the campaign to claims they intended to simply cut services. Labor MPs told their CHQ they wouldn't compromise their own integrity by using the privatisation rhetoric, which risked becoming a problem for Shorten late in the campaign. While direct phone calls by Labor operatives to low-information voters did harm the government on this issue, Shorten's early success in the free media was replaced by a bollocking because of the fraudulent nature of some of his attacks. That this criticism from the mainstream media did Shorten little harm may make Mediscare a landmark moment in Australian politics.

Nick Xenophon found himself with a similar problem in South Australia. He fronted a television spot, looking into the camera to say we 'won't be introducing a bill to reduce penalty rates'. Xenophon is more trusted than most politicians but the problem with this tactic was that the first time many voters heard about the issue would have been through Xenophon's own ad. It's hard playing defence in politics. The Howard government faced the same problem with their 'myth busting' advertisement rebutting accusations about WorkChoices. These efforts tend to reinforce rather than kill the charges made by opponents.

Labor strategists believed that the recent record of leaders at previous elections pledging not to do what they go on to do—Tony Abbott on a multitude of cuts, Julia Gillard on the carbon tax—would undermine Turnbull's denials of any plans to abolish Medicare. Labor peppered social media with Abbott's interview on SBS the night before the 2013 election when he had promised 'no cuts to education, no cuts to health, no changes to pensions, no change to the GST, and no cuts to the ABC and SBS'. The footage had been replayed endlessly as Abbott ticked off each broken promise in the first year of his government, although he left changing the GST to his successor (not that Turnbull had the mettle to do so). Labor followed up with a television spot that actually used Turnbull's response to its attack—'Medicare will never be privatised'—showing how difficult positive messaging can be when on the back foot. The Turnbull grab was shown after John Howard's 'never ever' declaration about a GST in 1996 and the Abbott SBS promises footage—a trifecta of untrustworthy Liberal leaders, Labor claimed. 'Liberals say one thing and do another' was the tag.

Labor at least ended the farce of opposition parties releasing their expected fiscal position days before the election. Its concession that it would run a larger deficit than that forecast by the government was announced by Bowen and finance spokesperson Tony Burke along with a 32-page 'ten-year' plan. Treasurer Scott Morrison mocked the lack of detail in the plan—final figures were to be released early in the last week of the campaign—and commentators questioned the wisdom of Labor conceding short-term fiscal virtue to the Coalition. When Morrison and finance minister Mathias Cormann called a media conference to condemn Labor's so-called $67-billion budget black hole, the stunt was widely seen to have backfired. Labor ridiculed the quantum of the figure, pointing out that it was 'tens of billions' of dollars off the mark, which implicitly admitted to a sizeable hole in its costings. The figure Morrison and Cormann arrived at included anything Labor had blocked during the life of the parliament, or indeed cuts it had criticised. The purpose of sticking to the imaginary $67 billion was to force Labor to clarify which cuts it had criticised but would nonetheless stick with in government, such as cuts to foreign aid and the end of the school-kids bonus.

Get Ready for Take-off

Shorten officially launched Labor's campaign in western Sydney with only three of the four living Labor prime ministers—Bob Hawke, Paul Keating and Julia Gillard—looking on. Kevin Rudd must have been busy prematurely lobbying for UN votes. Shorten's pitch that 'this election is a referendum on the future of Medicare', which had Turnbull, also campaigning in western Sydney, on the defensive, overshadowed solid Labor policy on domestic violence and Shorten's strongest denunciation to date of the same-sex marriage plebiscite. While Labor was likely to struggle to gain enough seats federally to win, New South Wales was looking promising.

Coalition MPs in western Sydney complained after the campaign that they hadn't been privy to polling showing voters turning against them. Swings of 4 per cent (Lindsay) and more than 6 per cent (Macquarie) weren't late reactions to Mediscare, though. Louise Markus had repeatedly asked Liberal headquarters for resources on the basis that her seat of Macquarie was under threat, to no avail. Fiona Scott, in the seat of Lindsay—where Shorten's launch was held—had declined to publicly say which leader got her vote in September 2015, but it was widely assumed that she had backed Turnbull. Abbott had strongly backed Scott in 2013, cringingly comparing her to John Howard favourite Jackie Kelly in that both had, among other things, 'sex appeal'. For that campaign,

Abbott had used resources from his safe seat of Warringah to help target Scott's marginal seat. These resources were withdrawn in 2016 due to the belief that Scott had voted for Turnbull, with local Liberal Party members in both Lindsay and Warringah refusing to help Scott's campaign. Not every marginal seat can be saved. The Coalition's campaign approach was a retention strategy—taking advantage of the 90 seats Abbott had delivered in 2013, sacrificing some seats in a bid to minimise overall losses. MPs who had their resource allocations pared back were alerted to this fact. Turnbull was a different type of leader to Howard and Abbott, who both did well in western Sydney. His social liberalism would pick up votes in areas closer to the capital cities, such as Brisbane, where two gay candidates for the two major parties made history, and in Chisholm in Melbourne, the only seat the Coalition would take from Labor.

Struggling to shake off both a cold virus and Mediscare, Turnbull needed a boost. He needed to combat a feeling within the Liberal Party that Abbott would have been far more effective on the hustings in attacking Shorten and shifting the free media's focus to strengths for the Coalition beyond just the economy. Abbott certainly would have had more energy than Turnbull displayed over the very long campaign. The Liberals had planned a low-key campaign launch, though, which wasn't about to reset the contest. It was held in the electorate of Reid, which wasn't even on Labor's radar as a marginal seat Team Shorten thought it could win. Abbott walked in with John Howard to ensure sustained applause, and Turnbull's tributes to the former prime ministers were closely bracketed to prevent the acclamation for Howard being measured against that for Abbott. It was shrewd politicking. The look on Abbott's face when Turnbull thanked him merely for putting the Rudd–Gillard government out of its misery, after lauding Howard for his government's achievements, was priceless. From the point of view of CHQ, the campaign was going well. Errors were kept to a minimum; internal research showed the government winning the election. 'The anger just isn't there any more,' one MP argued. '[Voters] are disappointed in Malcolm, but that's okay. They don't want to go back to Labor which is something they were genuinely considering before.' There were holes in the research, though, such as the fall in the Liberal vote in Tasmania.

Turnbull was not as adept as Shorten at maximising the free media. Labor had shown that its policy focus would be on health until election day. To the Coalition, this looked like a concession that Labor had abandoned the economic debate and therefore the election. By contrast, Labor strategists held that their own polling in marginal seats was closer than the publicly released polls, although they refused to give any details to journalists, and their view was that Shorten and Chris Bowen had done enough to neutralise the economic debate, and that their campaign on health tied in with Shorten's overall message on fairness.

The appearance of complacency in a leader, though, is never good. In a set speech to Paralympians, Turnbull looked tired, and his voice was starting to fade. The right balance is to appear confident but not arrogant, hoping voters will choose the stability of an incumbent government instead of lodging a protest in the expectation that the government would be returned. Both sides also agreed that Turnbull's credibility was central to a Coalition victory. This was a point Nutt and Textor focused on at their party-room briefing to MPs after the election. The two most played television spots featured Turnbull—Labor's arguing Turnbull was out of touch, the Coalition's using Turnbull to stress his central argument on jobs and growth. When Turnbull declared that he could win, Shorten accused him of arrogance. As had often been the case when Labor changed tactics during the campaign, not everyone followed the leader. Shorten's parliamentary secretary, Terri Butler, spruiked similar lines to Turnbull's, that Labor hoped to win, on the very same afternoon. Anthony Albanese had done similarly at the start of the campaign during an appearance on Sky News.

While the leaders were officially launching their campaigns, thousands of people were already voting. While the use of prepoll and postal votes is on the rise, with a record 2.5 million in this campaign, most such electors are not swinging voters, making them less susceptible to the vagaries of what made news on the day they lodged their votes.

Abbott was right that national security could have played a larger part in the campaign—even though Abbott meant primarily asylum-seekers rather than terrorism and defence policy. In addition to Dutton's outlandish attempt to link refugees with unemployment, there was some manufactured news on turn-backs of Vietnamese asylum-seekers, but this didn't generate much coverage outside the *Daily Telegraph*'s 'Boats Are Back' splash. Immigration Minister Peter Dutton declined to hold an inquiry into how the *Tele* got the classified information about on-water matters. As Dutton observed after the election, 'in part we were a victim of our own success … essentially the issue had gone off the radar'. Broader security issues didn't feature once the South Australian submarine decision received bipartisan support. Days after a Muslim gunman slaughtered dozens of people at a gay nightclub in Orlando, Florida, Turnbull marked the end of Ramadan with a multi-faith dinner. Sheikh Shady Alsuleiman, whose record of calling for the death penalty for homosexuality was easy enough to google, made the guest list. Turnbull expressed regret for having issued the invitation, but the damage was done and the delcons were presented with an error by Turnbull—on a silver platter—that Abbott never would have made.

All of this was displaced, though, by a genuine problem when the people of the United Kingdom voted to leave the European Union. The vote spelled the end of David Cameron's leadership—a sign that trying to solve internal problems with a public vote can go in unexpected directions. The financial ructions following the vote drew attention to Turnbull's emphasis on stability. The man whose entire prime ministership was a giant gamble warned voters at his campaign launch that a vote for Labor, minor parties or independents was 'a role of the dice'. Nationals leader Barnaby Joyce met the challenge from Tony Windsor in New England by warning of the return of the Labor–Greens–independent alliance. Within weeks Turnbull adopted similar rhetoric. After the UK Brexit vote, he told Tasmanians, 'It's a very clear choice. A stable government—

a majority Coalition Government which I lead with a clear national economic plan already delivering economic growth and more jobs across Australia and here in Tasmania—or the chaos of a Labor–Greens–independent alliance.'

The first Newspoll after the Brexit vote, while moving within the margin error, added to the perception that momentum was behind the government. It turned out not to be true. A Shorten win would have required a series of firsts. With Newspoll showing his approval rating at 30 per cent, he would have become the winner with the lowest rating in the history of that poll—and the highest dissatisfaction rating. Turnbull's ratings weren't much better but he was a known, if not fully understood, quantity. Labor's primary vote at 36 per cent in Newspoll, even given the policy of harvesting plenty of preferences, had historically been too low to win.

The final week saw Shorten come under fire for costings inconsistencies and misuse of rhetoric designed to label Turnbull as untrustworthy. The nightly news that followed saw all the heavy hitters come down hard on the opposition leader.

In contrast the prime minister gave a strong, albeit boringly on message, performance at the National Press Club, where he stuck to his messages on the economy and stability, especially in the wake of the Brexit vote. Not that the government's record on the economy was all that good. Turnbull positioned himself in the sensible middle ground. 'I believe they want our parliament to offload the ideology, to end the juvenile theatrics and gotcha moments, to drop the personality politics,' he told the Press Club. 'They want our focus to be on issues that matter to them—and an end to division for division's sake. Australians are entitled to expect that of their parliament.' John Howard reminded all and sundry of the importance of Turnbull winning a large enough majority to pass bills at a joint sitting. Depending on the composition of the Senate, this would be around 82 seats in the House of Representatives—a loss of just 8 and well within Labor's reach.

Labor highlighted examples of GPs abandoning bulk-billing. Turnbull was nervous enough about the result on election eve to make a promise that may prove reminiscent of Abbott's 2013 effort. Asked on Channel 7 whether he could guarantee that nobody would have to pay more to visit a doctor because of the government's freeze on Medicare payments, Turnbull unhesitatingly replied, 'Absolutely.' Realising the potential for damage, Turnbull fronted the cameras again later in the day to suggest that it was up to doctors whether or not they increased fees, but the public couldn't blame the government if they did.

Closing Arguments

The longest election campaign in modern Australian history was punctuated by tactical victories to Bill Shorten and the Labor opposition. Shorten was better at winning the daily media battles, and using 'announceables' to dominate the free news coverage. He also showed more agility—which is interesting, given that 'agility' is one of Turnbull's favourite words—in fronting up for interviews across multiple media platforms, and more enthusiasm for the often trying task of feigning interest in the activities of fellow Australians. That said, Shorten largely avoided the long-form interview lest his superficial campaign be exposed. Turnbull was a much better campaigner after eight weeks on the job. Boosted by internal polling, he grew in confidence in the last two weeks, though he was thwarted by Labor's Mediscare campaign.

Late in the campaign the two biggest challenges saw contrasting concerns for the major parties. Shorten was forced to fend off stories about his future after an electoral defeat, which is the ultimate distraction for an opposition leader still trying to win an election. Turnbull's challenge was containing expectations. The polls were tight throughout, so the risk of a protest vote against the government remained constant. The last thing Turnbull wanted to expose the government to was defeat by stealth—the public giving the Coalition a long-overdue kick in the pants that accidentally also kicked them out of government after just one term. That hasn't been the fate of any federal government since way back in 1931.

Neither prime-ministerial candidate broke from the recent past of uninspiring rhetoric, cautious engagement with issues and limited debating skills. It's hard to know whom or what to blame for this enduring trend. Yes, the political class appears weaker than it once was, partly because it is a less diverse place in terms of the occupational background of MPs.[3] Fewer members come from outside the party machine. But the media and voters are also to blame for lacklustre campaigns. Trivial reporting feeds into cautious campaigning, and voter disengagement doesn't drive quality debating of ideas. While there is a chicken-and-egg argument to be had as to what came first—the disengaged voter or the uninspiring politician—either way the public aren't demanding more of their politicians by tuning in and calling them to account.

Instead, people have further disengaged, with ever lowering expectations about what the political class is capable of delivering. Essential Research found that 14 per cent of voters made up their mind in the last week. All up, the result was in line with the minimum expectations for the Turnbull backers. They had won a majority government. A clearer result on election night probably would have helped the spin in the days that followed.

It wasn't just the delcons who thought the campaign themes were poorly conceived. Rowan Ramsay, whose seat comprises most of regional South Australia, found little resonance among his voters from Turnbull's jobs and growth message. Most commentary, including the draft of this chapter, assumed that Turnbull would win with a reduced but comfortable majority. In the end it was anything but comfortable. The belief that Labor couldn't gain enough seats to win turned out to be true. The Coalition scare campaign about minority government was well founded. As commentators killed time on election day speculating how many seats Turnbull would win by, voters were composing another twist in the tale of Australia's tumultuous contemporary politics. If the 2016 campaign was unmemorable, it was capped by an election night that few would forget.

Eight
YOU HAD ONE JOB

TEMPERS HAD ALREADY frayed by the time the votes were counted, with a scuffle between volunteers at one Melbourne polling booth, and partisans debating the campaign on television panels. In his testy address to Liberal supporters after midnight, Turnbull said he expected police to investigate a text message to voters claiming to be from Medicare—one of the more bizarre pieces of information to emerge in an election-night speech. Turnbull twice invoked John Howard, having embraced the former prime minister on his way to the podium. The two had spoken on the telephone earlier in the evening. Howard, at least, had been transformed since the republic debate from villain to crutch. Turnbull returned to the Australian Building and Construction Commission and the Construction Forestry Mining and Energy Union, perhaps only drawing attention to the fact that he hadn't said a lot about either over the long election campaign. Those still in the room after midnight reported that the speech was well received, but that shouldn't have been Turnbull's focus.

Turnbull misjudged the tone his speech needed to strike, just as Paul Keating had in 1993, albeit under quite different circumstances.

Keating, the unexpected victor, declared the result 'the sweetest victory of all'. The faithful might have felt that way, but not the voters, who found it difficult to embrace either side of politics at that time. On Turnbull's watch, what Australians wanted, post-election polls found, was reassurance that their health system was safe, which Turnbull did not provide.

Delcon-in-chief Andrew Bolt wasted no time in calling on Turnbull to resign early on in the night. Conservatives admitted to us that they were cheering on the government losses on election night, notwithstanding the number of conservative MPs who had lost their jobs. The inevitable question of whether Tony Abbott would have done better than Turnbull would only reinforce negative perceptions of Abbott in the minds of most Liberal MPs. They had made their judgement about that question in September 2015 and decided that the gamble was worth taking. While there were no guarantees on election night, with close counting to continue in a number of seats for days, it seemed likely the Turnbull gamble had succeeded. Replacing Abbott with Turnbull had delivered the Coalition majority government and a second term. But only after one hell of a fright.

The close result was jarring for Turnbull. Following him during the last week of the campaign, journalist Tony Wright had observed 'a casual and confident spring in his step'. None of Turnbull's staff had given him reason to dent his confidence. Early results confirmed the party polling. However, very soon into the count all three Liberal seats in Tasmania looked lost. This result blindsided Liberal Party CHQ, which had expected to hold on to at least two of the three seats. As Laurie Oakes fed more of Turnbull's colleagues through Channel Nine's animated 'crusher' and onto the political scrapheap, the leader was inconsolable. The prospect of another hung parliament, leadership instability, gridlock in the Senate and a resurgent opposition put enormous pressure on Turnbull in the days after the election. Had some of the seats that later fell into the Coalition column been called on the night of the main count, some of the panic would have been avoided and the carping of the delcons would have had less credibility.

After the speech Turnbull and his inner circle retreated to a pre-booked suite in the hotel to have a few drinks and try to absorb what had just happened. It was the first point in the night the PM started to relax. It wasn't until the Tuesday after Saturday's election that Turnbull accepted responsibility for the campaign:

> There is no doubt that there is a level of disillusionment with politics, with government, and with the major parties. Our own included. We note that. We respect it. Now, we need to listen very carefully to the concerns of the Australian people expressed through this election. We need to look at how we will address those concerns.

He wouldn't let go of the idea that Mediscare was unfair but conceded that health would be a policy area where things may have to change.

The two Liberal MPs who suffered the biggest swings against them, Russell Matheson in Macarthur and Anthony Nikolic in Bass, had both voted for Abbott—Nikolic very publicly so as government whip. Perhaps there was something admirable in the three Tasmanian Liberals sticking with Abbott even though they knew their seats were under threat, or maybe they were resigned to their fate. Turnbull did help Abbott supporter Ann Sudmalis win a tight contest in Gilmore. Bert van Manen probably saved his seat of Forde by backing Turnbull. And the Liberal Party certainly would not have retained the seat of Brisbane had it not been for the change of leader. Along with Peter Hendy and Wyatt Roy, Luke Simpkins, one of the first backbenchers to call for a leadership spill in 2015, wasn't so lucky in his seat of Cowan. Ken Wyatt in nearby Hasluck voted for Turnbull and did save his seat. In the Victorian seat of Chisholm, the only seat the government won off the opposition, Liberal candidate Julia Banks declined a polite offer from Abbott to join her on the campaign trail. She took the view that her best chance was to keep the former PM out of her electorate, given the polling problems Liberals had in Victoria prior to the leadership change. Abbott joined Karen McNamara in her seat of Dobell and Natasha Griggs in Solomon in the Northern Territory. Both reportedly voted for Abbott, but neither was lucky enough to retain their seat. Abbott's electoral conference was supposed to provide financial assistance to Fiona Scott in her marginal western suburbs seat of Lindsay, but because she voted for Turnbull that support was withdrawn and she lost the seat. The Nationals easily won Liberal Sharman Stone's former seat of Murray, reversing a long trend of Liberals winning such three-cornered contests. The junior Coalition partner proved more successful than the Liberals in defending its own seats. It actually netted one additional lower-house seat once the counting was completed.

Polls showed that the changes to superannuation shifted few votes from the Coalition. Still, Turnbull would have to be careful in managing the issue, since it had negatively impacted on fundraising and volunteer assistance on polling day. The average swing from Nationals and Liberals to Labor was almost the same. Post-election news stories defied each of these facts. While Turnbull was absorbing blows from commentators and his own team, Bill Shorten took a lap of honour around the country to thank voters for … another three years in opposition. It was an over-the-top performance. It was only when Shorten finally rang Turnbull to concede defeat that the loss sank in for him. Three more years on the wrong side of the treasury benches was his reward for a better than expected showing.

While Bill Shorten worked very hard in the aftermath of the election to suggest that there was no threat to his leadership and Labor remained united, in truth the final week of the campaign saw both left and right factions make early preparations for what to do with the opposition leader in the event of a poor showing. The NSW right was weighing up a shift to Anthony Albanese, with a longer-term plan for either Chris Bowen or Tony Burke to emerge as the next Labor prime minister. A month out from the election, Albanese set up a very different set of key performance indicators to those Shorten wanted used when on *Australian Agenda* on Sky News he pointed out that Labor was ahead in the polls, had the momentum and expected to win the election. In other words, if Labor lost it would be because Shorten's campaign failed, neatly setting up a leadership challenge. Remember, 55 per cent of Labor's membership had wanted Albanese as leader three years ago.

Victorian right-wing powerbrokers had no plans to desert Shorten, but they worried about their NSW right colleagues. They even doubted the chances of the right holding its membership together if they factionally fell in behind Shorten one more time. Shorten knew all of this was going on, so he tried to shore up the NSW right with late election announceables directed at the post-election circus rather than winning votes. Albanese for his part had every intention of running against Shorten, even though he avoided answering questions on the subject during the campaign. 'Fight the Tories first then worry about the Labor leadership' was his mantra.

The Liberals got word of what was going on behind the scenes within Labor, which gave them what turned out to be a misplaced faith in their capacity to retain seats. Team Shorten successfully managed to keep the focus on Medicare at the same time as lowering expectations. It contrasted sharply with Team Turnbull, which didn't do enough to manage expectations that a late surge might see the government only lose a handful of seats. This worsened the political fallout for Turnbull in the immediate aftermath of the election. Meanwhile, Shorten had little to worry about once the results showed how well Labor had done, even in defeat. The plan among Shorten detractors had been to use a seats showing of less than 70 against him, but that didn't happen. Labor fell one short of that number with a woeful primary vote, but it mattered not. The story was the government being unable to claim victory for a week as counting continued, taking the pressure off Shorten. He called for a caucus meeting while the votes were still being counted, without having conceded defeat, so as to be re-confirmed as Labor leader. Albo was snookered, and hence moved the motion for Shorten.

The narrative Labor sought to push following the election focused on the notion of chaos and dysfunction in government ranks, courtesy of the large swathe of seats Turnbull lost. A closer look provides a more nuanced understanding. With the exception of the Nationals, no established major or minor party can be satisfied with the results. Majority government is better than what the Coalition was looking at before it changed leaders. Thirty consecutive Newspolls in arrears don't lie. An autocratic leader and an even more autocratic Prime Ministerial Office didn't instil confidence. Throw in a PM with a tin ear and no wonder Liberals did the unthinkable last September. They didn't shift and go all-in on a former leader who had failed in 2009 because they thought they were going to win the election under Abbott, let's put it that way. A Galaxy poll one week out from the election hypothesised about Abbott leading the government, with the consequence being a massive dip in the Coalition's vote.

Two weeks after the election, with votes still being counted in the seat of Herbert, Coalition MPs and those waiting for the agonising Senate count gathered in Canberra. Turnbull held a victory celebration at The Lodge. Abbott missed out on the canapés, having a prior commitment with his mother. Indeed, about a third of MPs had a reason to stay away. The mood was surprisingly upbeat, given the number of seats lost and how close the government had come to losing its majority. One factor of course was that the vanquished didn't secure an invite—returned MPs only. There wasn't much by way of backbiting and 'getting shit off the liver' as one MP put it to us. Planning for such an eventuality was part of the PM's thinking in having the function—as a way of lessening criticisms in the more formal party-room setting. If MPs had points they wanted to make Turnbull hoped they would be more pointed that evening rather than in the party room when conversations are heard by all and often dutifully reported back to press-gallery journalists on the hunt for a story. 'No one really had a crack at what went wrong from what I heard,' one MP present said. 'Perhaps the jovial mood helped ease tensions, I don't know. But it wasn't a case of getting things off anyone's chests. Colleagues who might have been inclined to do that weren't there anyway.'

The next morning at a joint party-room meeting, Turnbull invited the cameras in to see the smiling faces as he revved up the troops. This occurred at the start of the meeting, before the doors were closed and the free and frank discussion really got underway. Turnbull still wished to deflect blame from himself—highlighting Mediscare and the lack of regulation of robo calls and text messages as means of campaigning. Tony Nutt and Mark Textor gave their campaign debriefs, minus any self-criticisms that would have been appropriate. Nutt reiterated his view that the leadership change on balance saved seats but that voters had begun to lose confidence in the government from the beginning of the year. Textor defended the balance between positive and negative messaging. He noted the cynicism of voters in western Sydney, which made any type of persuasion about politics difficult. They were primed for Labor's cynical approach to Medicare. He argued that the economic debate had shifted in recent elections towards uncertainty about jobs. Textor was surprised to receive applause at the end of his address, a sign that he was nervous as to how MPs and senators would respond to his defence of the campaign tactics, which had been publicly criticised.

Only Eric Abetz raised the superannuation issue, partly as a defensive ploy to help explain the dismal performance of his own division. Others who had raised concerns publicly did not do so in the party room. Nor did Nationals MP George Christensen, who subsequently said that he would cross the floor if changes weren't made to the policy. Former SAS officer Andrew Hastie, who had condemned the central tactics used in the campaign as not suited to his own seat, didn't feel the need to reiterate what he had told the media once inside the party room. Courage comes in different forms. Perhaps the most unhelpful observation from the floor came from Senator Ian Macdonald, who took the opportunity to criticise the 'early' party-room meeting 'disrespecting' senators who were yet to be confirmed by the count. They weren't there and thus missed out on their opportunity to have a say on the leadership, he said. The look from Turnbull said it all. Another MP pointed out the leadership positions weren't being contested, so what did it matter?

Turnbull baulked at his first tough decision after the election. With the Nationals increasing their proportion of Coalition MPs and therefore of the ministry, he increased the size of the cabinet instead of disappointing ambitious Liberals. Conservatives Josh Frydenberg, Zed Seselja, Fiona Nash and Matt Canavan were promoted. Scott Ryan resumed his role as assistant minister to the cabinet secretary, also adding the outer ministerial position of special minister of state to his list of titles.

Christopher Pyne was made responsible for defence procurement within the defence ministry—'minister for Adelaide'. In a government that took defence seriously, such a senior figure in the cabinet would take on the strategic defence role—not the one responsible for handing out money. Greg Hunt had lobbied to move to the trade portfolio when Turnbull reshuffled his frontbench previously, but was overlooked for Steve Ciobo. This time the environment minister finally got to move out of a portfolio he had been stuck in across a multitude of leadership changes in government and opposition. Hunt moved into the industry, innovation and science space, which pleased him greatly. Internal tensions were papered over by a larger ministry at taxpayers' expense.

It didn't take long for Labor to start brawling over the spoils of opposition, with Albanese's attempt to remove Victorian left warrior Kim Carr from the shadow ministery thwarted by Shorten. Carr was an important Shorten ally against Albanese, so he had to be saved. Meanwhile, there was only room for the best economic brain in the parliament, Andrew Leigh, due to an increase in the size of the shadow ministry. Leigh took on added responsibilities but with a pay cut to go with it. Legislation limits to thirty the number of shadow ministers eligible for the $40,000 salary increase MPs get when sitting on the frontbench, and Leigh didn't make the list determined by the factions. Shorten saved him but not his salary—one of the former AWU national secretary's worst negotiated settlements on behalf of workers.

A swift decision to establish a royal commission into youth detention in the Northern Territory in response to a *Four Corners* report featuring horrifying images of abuse was understandable but also a sign of the pressures facing the re-elected prime minister. Whether the Royal Commission was established in days rather than hours it seemed to be more about the media cycle than the demands of sound decision-making. In the weeks after the election Turnbull was also under pressure over how to deal with the banks and a botched national Census. Shorten played politics with the royal commission when he made his first public comments since the shocking images had appeared on television five days earlier. Shorten publicly called for two indigenous co-commissioners to play a role in the proceedings. It was an excellent idea, but one that should have been communicated privately to the government, if the aim was to achieve an outcome rather than a headline, that is. Turnbull's haste was underlined when his first-choice commissioner stepped aside and was replaced by joint indigenous and non-indigenous choices.

Public divisions over something as trivial as whether Kevin Rudd would be nominated for secretary-general of the United Nations also filled the vacuum with parliament not set to return for nearly two months after the election. Rudd proved his unsuitability for the role, despite having the perfect CV for it, by releasing details of private correspondence with the PM after his disappointment was realised. Not the most democratic course of action for a wannabe secretary-general.

Judging the Turnbull Gamble

Had majority government been guaranteed when the decision was made to oust Abbott in September 2015, even with a slender majority, you can bet Liberal MPs would have accepted. Individual marginal-seat MPs who voted for Turnbull would have backed themselves not to be among the dozen or so who would go on to lose their seats. Besides, many already felt that such an outcome was likely if Abbott stayed leader. Turnbull's biggest problem became expectations management, as the national relief following Abbott's removal was replaced by inflated hopes soon dashed.

A minority government of course is another matter entirely: it's doubtful the Liberals would have rolled Abbott so unceremoniously, unleashing a vicious response from conservative commentators, if they'd thought Turnbull could deliver only minority government. So the difference between the Coalition's winning 75 and 76 seats in the House of Representatives is the key factor when assessing whether or not the Turnbull gamble was, as a minimum yardstick, a success.

Still, the Turnbull gamble had delivered a Pyrrhic victory to the Coalition in the eyes of some. The way that election night unfolded affected perceptions of Turnbull's performance, and perceptions matter in politics. After the dust had settled, *The Australian*'s David Crowe wrote that for Turnbull 'to surrender on the super tax increases would be to wipe out what is left of his authority after he took the government close to disaster at the election'. Transaction cost number one: short memories. Turnbull, not Abbott, was the one who took the government close to disaster.

Nevertheless, Turnbull is the author of his own fortunes as the occupant of the nation's highest office. Commentators railed against Turnbull's unwillingness to become whatever it was that they imagined him to be. Voters, many of whom might have approved of the leadership change without ever planning to vote for the Coalition, shared this disappointment in the new prime minister. Journalist Paul Bongiorno saw the May 2016 budget as 'Turnbull's biggest opportunity to show that he is finally his own man, prepared to throw off the shackles of the Abbott framework that has seen his standing in the broader electorate come crashing down.' It wasn't the ghost of Abbott that restricted Turnbull's options, though. It was his supporters not his enemies that had boxed him in. That was the price of power.

A wafer-thin majority dependent on disciplined voting from the likes of Tony Abbott and Kevin Andrews may surprise with its success. Crossing the floor when a majority isn't at stake is easy in the Coalition parties. Doing it while costing the government a majority is a much more serious risk. Modern political history tells us that first-term federal governments don't lose elections, but they often come close. In 2010 Julia Gillard scraped home after forming a minority government. In 1998 John Howard's government lost 14 seats—a similar number to Turnbull's—and retained office with only 49 per cent of the two-party vote. Even a popular Bob Hawke went backwards against Andrew Peacock at the 1984 election. Turnbull won a majority of the seats and a majority of the popular vote, and kept Labor's primary vote well below where it should be. Seen in this context, and against the backdrop of Abbott's regular stumbles, office mismanagement and long-term failure in the polls, it's no wonder that most who voted to change prime ministers consider the Turnbull gamble a success.

In a sign of the internal fights to come, senior government figures were quick to argue that Abbott would have performed worse at the election than Turnbull did. That is probably right. He was a less popular figure, and the Medicare scare campaign would have been even more potent against Abbott than it was against Turnbull. It is impossible to prove a hypothetical alternative, though, and the Abbott conservatives can retort that the former PM was a proven campaigner. Then there are the unknowns. What were the transaction costs for voters in the switch? Did they outweigh the benefits of offloading such an unpopular PM? Would Abbott have avoided some of the policy blunders Turnbull stumbled into over the last eight months? He certainly would have targeted Bill Shorten's negatives more strongly.

The Turnbull gamble had an added yardstick for judging success by the ability to hold a joint sitting to pass the ABCC laws, given that they were the trigger for the early double-dissolution election. John Howard told Sky News during the campaign that Turnbull would be judged on his capacity to deliver both outcomes. Once the results had come in, however, he told Liberals not to 'slit their wrists'.

This parliament will require the government to navigate another difficult Senate, and the politicking of obstruction and populism creates the sort of potent mix that isn't likely to help efforts to get the budget under control. Shorten has mastered the art of requesting bipartisanship, but only on his terms. More debt and fewer chances to cut government spending await any treasurer seeking to craft the national accounts. The government's AAA credit rating won't last long under such circumstances. What motivated the electorate to issue the government such a sharp repudiation?

Undoubtedly, Labor's disingenuous scare campaign on Medicare resonated with the electorate. It fomented doubts about a government that had already underwhelmed voters. It solidified distrust in the Coalition's intentions on healthcare in the wake of cuts and co-payments sought in the 2014 budget. Concentrating on Labor's dishonesty over Medicare prevented any reflection on why the strategy was so effective. Few in the Liberal Party seemed willing to do what Howard had done after the 1993 defeat, when he accepted that public support for Medicare was a cornerstone of contemporary politics. Funding health was easier for Howard during the mining boom. In the days after the 2016 election, treasurer Scott Morrison kept to the campaign script of extracting greater value from planned spending levels, emphasising that health could not become a 'money pit'.

Turnbull will need to manage two key issues during this term of government—the threat of internal divisions within the Liberal Party, sparked by personality and ideological feuds, and the policy challenges the nation faces. These are inextricably linked. Without unity, policy scripts won't even get to the stage of being put before a difficult Senate, much less negotiated into legislative outcomes. And if failures of policy process or design do emerge, they will certainly stoke internal tensions. The forty-fifth parliament will be a difficult one, but it doesn't have to be as hard to navigate as the forty-third parliament was for Julia Gillard. Those were truly difficult times, in the wake of the unprecedented move of ousting first-term PM Rudd, only to slide back into office as a minority government.

To be sure, achieving major initiatives will be harder for Turnbull. Even though Gillard's Labor Party was in minority government, in conjunction with the Greens she controlled the Senate. Once the lower-house crossbenchers were on board, the rest was mere formality. Gillard's cross to bear was the perception of dysfunction, made worse by the undermining she faced from Rudd supporters and the relentless attacks from Abbott. Turnbull will face the conservative equivalent of what Rudd unleashed if he can't win over the next generation. But perceptions of parliamentary dysfunction can be contained, at least so far as the lower house is concerned. Turnbull has a working majority, as well as pledges of support from a number of crossbenchers occupying traditionally right-of-centre electorates. A key reason Gillard's government was painted as dysfunctional was her regular meetings with the Greens and the perception she was beholden to the likes of independents Tony Windsor and Rob Oakeshott. Turnbull's majority will come in handy for avoiding such an outcome but his own decision to use a double dissolution will make the Senate as difficult to negotiate with as any in memory. Senates have always been more volatile than lower houses, at least stretching back to the introduction of proportional representation reforms in 1948–49. To be successful in this term, Turnbull can't let Shorten use upper-house horse trading or obstruction to paint the Coalition as dysfunctional. This will be a key battleground in the coming months and years.

Equally, if the next generation of conservatives can learn to live with a party led by Turnbull, at least for a while, the ranting and raving of a few shouldn't cause wider dysfunction. Parliamentary party rooms are like extended families—there are always a few malcontents in the ranks. Beyond Abbott, Kevin Andrews, Eric Abetz and Cory Bernardi, it is hard to establish anyone else within the parliamentary Liberal Party deeply loathing of Turnbull as PM. Plenty couldn't reasonably be counted as card-carrying supporters, and even more have their doubts about his political skills in holding the show together. But such worries don't immediately translate into open hostility, or moves to find a better alternative. Expect the disaffected ageing conservatives—'Dad's Army'—to take advantage of their mentoring roles to a younger generation of conservatives, as has happened to Andrew Hastie with the poor advice and cheering on he received for publicly criticising the campaign and challenging his prime minister on policy scripts. Without a hint of irony, Abbott's former chief of staff Peta Credlin used a column a week after the election to praise Hastie for speaking his mind when he lampooned the campaign strategy before the result of the election was known. 'She'd have torn him limb from limb had he pulled that stunt when Tony was PM, former SAS officer or not,' one MP who voted for Abbott in both spills wryly noted. But so long as the likes of Peter Dutton, Mathias Cormann, Christian Porter and Josh Frydenberg remain in the upper echelons of the government, and are listened to, the trickle-down effect should keep a new generation of conservatives happy. The right mix of ministerial promotions will help. These conservatives will have to be listened to, not bought off.

When interviewed on the ABC on the night of the leadership challenge in 2015, Arthur Sinodinos made a lot of Turnbull's learning curve over the previous six years. He likened Turnbull's journey to that of John Howard, who came back into the Liberal leadership with a fresh outlook on factional deal-making and consultation. In truth, Howard's learning curve steepened even further once he won office, and the pay-off only really set in after a difficult re-election in 1998, when the Coalition won less than 49 per cent of the national vote, even if Howard's government won a few more seats than Turnbull's. Howard won with a stronger agenda than that of Turnbull, and he confronted an easier-to-manage Senate. But what made the 1998–2001 Howard government a success was a mixture of policy implementation, internal stability and a little luck. Labor made the mistake of assuming it was a government-in-waiting after its strong 1998 performance—an easy mistake for a relatively new opposition still dominated by former ministers to make.

While the Turnbull gamble achieved its baseline of winning a majority in the House of Representatives, to really pay off Turnbull must now govern effectively. Voters don't want much: stability, reassurance in areas such as health policy, and a pathway back to budget balance. If internal divisions can be minimised—a big if—three years in office would give Turnbull the time to prove he has no plans to dismantle Medicare. Any policy adjustments to accentuate this point would help win the argument. Spending restraint should enable Scott Morrison to deliver consecutive budgets that drive down the deficit, however slowly. If growth forecasts don't come in as expected, he'll have to make some tough decisions, but at the end of three years if debt has ebbed, that'll probably be enough for voters. There's not a lot of ambition in such an agenda, and it won't inspire those who had high expectations for Turnbull, but it would neatly contrast with Labor's plans to spend more. Stability, or the perception of stability, is the most important goal for a Coalition leader. In the current context it will also be the hardest to achieve.

Desire for stability after a tumultuous decade is likely to still be on voters' minds come 2019, so long as the Liberal leader can in fact point to the first full term for a prime minister since Howard's end. Especially if the alternative prime minister is still Bill Shorten. But it can be hard keeping a party room together with suicide bombers present. Turnbull's challenge will be to talk them down, or put them down in a way that keeps next-generation conservatives on side. Turnbull must either accept that he leads a party that is more conservative than he is, giving up all hope of performing better for his small-l liberal supporters, or start being himself and prosecuting the case for scripts that conservatives won't necessarily like. The latter option will likely unleash rounds of destabilisation, not just among conservative Liberals but from within the Nationals as well. A narrow majority is no mandate to radically unpick what it means to be in the modern Liberal Party, even if that definition has become more conservative relative to today's societal values than was the case in Menzies' day. While Nationals MPs might not get a formal say in leadership showdowns, they do influence colleagues, and they can certainly prop up or bring undone leaders. Abbott's fate was sealed when he lost the backing of Barnaby Joyce—the Nationals leader-in-waiting who went on to exceed all expectations at the 2016 election.

The opportunity Turnbull must seize is to define what it is to be a modern conservative away from the attempts by hard-right elements within the faction to shift the meaning of the word. Abbott is hanging around for one reason only—to influence this looming contest of ideas. For all his faults as a leader, he is no bower bird when it comes to philosophical principles, certainly not in his post-leadership phase. Abbott will be a formidable ideological opponent to Turnbull, all the more so, given the number of issues Turnbull will need to simultaneously manage as prime minister. John Howard always used to say that conservatives must dominate the ranks of the Liberal Party, as long as liberals are being listened to. It's questionable, of course, whether he followed his own script or merely paid lip service to it. This might be the very schism Turnbull advocates can exploit. Most Liberal Party members continue to revere Howard. Separating such partisans from those who wish the party harm under Turnbull's leadership may be the best way to ensure the Turnbull gamble pays off into the longer term, rather than merely locking in three more years in power when defeat looked on the cards.

It is arguable that what divides liberals and conservatives is becoming increasingly pronounced in the modern world. Pragmatism brings them into conflict even on economic matters, depending on who is residing in The Lodge. Social issues are a major area of disagreement, and this is a theatre that conservatives within the Liberal Party are increasingly looking to make the central focus. With Abbott involved that's no surprise.

One aspect of the election result is certain to reopen a longstanding debate within the Liberal Party. The proportion of Coalition women in the house went backwards from 20 per cent to 16 per cent in the first election after the Liberal federal executive established a target of 50 per cent representation by 2026. Only thirteen of the seventy-six MPs in the lower house for the Coalition are women. The comparison with Labor is now embarrassing, with Labor's proportion of women in the house edging above 40 per cent. Julie Bishop pointed out that a better overall result for the Coalition parties would have substantially increased the proportion of women. That is precisely why women need better access to the safer seats.

The party will have to seriously consider quotas if the difference is not to become even more embarrassing. Evidence from the business world suggests that even with the best of intentions, unless someone is accountable for achieving a set quota, targets will go unmet.[1] Turnbull began to correct one of Abbott's great failures when he promoted more women to the frontbench. However, having learned from the difficulties he faced when it came to candidate selection in 2009, Turnbull was on the sidelines as the number of women preselected for winnable seats fell. Liberals generally, including many Liberal women, don't like affirmative action. Female representation becomes obvious in parliament. When Coalition women look across the chamber on every sitting day they will have plenty of time to think about the virtues of quotas.

Pray for the Health of Coalition MPs

Voters wanted something different out of Australian politics but looked set to get more of the same after the 2016 election. Turnbull's leadership style has improved, but maybe not enough to overcome the challenges he now faces. Unlike Abbott, Turnbull seems capable of learning from his mistakes. He has been more consultative and less condescending to his colleagues. His political judgement, though, remains flawed, and what advice he is getting doesn't seem to be improving matters. A double-dissolution election with an interminable campaign was a poor decision. Going early would have been fine; going late would have been fine; the long campaign made the middle option the worst option. This was one occasion where Turnbull's instinct for a late election would have served him better than consulting his team.

Turnbull's future is in his party's own hands. Divided they will fall—as Gillard's minority government did. Find a way to stay united and show a level of governing competency we haven't seen for years, and the Turnbull gamble might just pay off beyond a narrow election win. Shorten is showing all the signs of seeking to emulate Abbott by wrecking the joint, but it is unclear if voters will reward such a strategy second time around, especially if the government doesn't descend into backbiting. State governments have shown that governing with slight majorities can lead to big wins at following elections, but that's without the intense scrutiny national politics receives. Federally, Menzies won the 1961 election with the barest of majorities—62 seats in the 122-seat lower house—going on to win comfortably at the following election. But politics was very different back then, and like modern state politics the scrutiny wasn't as intense as it is federally today. At one level the lack of a big agenda suits Turnbull's bower bird tendencies, even if he'd like to be remembered for major achievements. The Senate will make legislating initiatives difficult, but if infrastructure needs are placed at the heart of the government's focus, many such projects and plans do not require legislation. Wherever the government can notch up wins without fights in the Senate it must look to do so—regulation more than legislation will be Turnbull's friend over the next three years, if he lasts that long.

It's difficult to avoid the conclusion, though, that Turnbull simply doesn't deliver in an institutional environment. He was a dynamic journalist, barrister and entrepreneur, and could build respectful relationships with powerful employers such as Kerry Packer. However, whenever he has been responsible for leading a team—the Australian Republican Movement, Goldman Sachs, the Liberal Party and the Australian Government—the results have been underwhelming. In government, Turnbull wanted to be a transformational leader but lacked the time and the mandate to transform anything. A purely transactional approach would have delivered a stronger victory but would not have been authentically Turnbull. A year into his prime ministership, one of the most brilliant people to lead Australia has not been able to achieve much. This is consistent with the pattern of his life. Turnbull is not a team man, but he now has the challenge of leading a team under the most challenging of circumstances.

SOURCES

Sources have been provided where quotations are from books and articles not easily searchable, where the quotation is from an interview with the authors and the source is not clear from the text, where we give credit to a source not quoted, and to indicate further reading. Sources have not been provided where quotations were widely published and easily available online.

Prologue

1 See Wayne Errington and Peter van Onselen, *Battleground: Why the Liberal Party Shirtfronted Tony Abbott*, Melbourne University Press, Carlton, 2015, for a detailed examination of the factors that led to Abbott's demise, as well as some of the positioning that Turnbull and his supporters engaged in prior to challenging Abbott.

Introduction

1 *Australian Agenda*, Sky News Australia, 5 June 2016.

2 On the role of leaders' debates in election campaigns, see Philip Senior, 'Electoral Impact of Televised Debates', *Australian Journal of Political Science*, vol. 43, no. 3, 2008, pp. 434–64.

One—Transaction Costs: Past and Present

1 David Spicer, 'AFP Wins Access to James Ashby's Phone Records in Mal Brough Investigation,' ABC Online, 19 May 2016, http://www.abc.net.au/news/2016-05-19/afp-wins-access-to-james-ashby-phone-records/7427832 (viewed 30 July 2016).

2 The other two were Senators Mathias Cormann from Western Australia and Queenslander Brett Mason. The three penned a resignation letter to Turnbull and released it to the media.

3 Malcolm Turnbull, *The Spycatcher Trial*, Mandarin Australia, Melbourne, 1987, p. 2.
4 Steve Kilbey, *Something Quite Peculiar*, Hardie Grant Books, Melbourne, 2014.
5 Cited in Paddy Manning, *Born to Rule: The Unauthorised Biography of Malcolm Turnbull*, Melbourne University Press, Carlton, 2015.
6 David H Barlow and V Mark Durand, *Abnormal Psychology: An Integrative Approach*, 3rd edn, Wadsworth, Belmont, 2002, p. 10.
7 See, for example, John Lyons, 'Raging Turnbull', *Good Weekend*, 13 April 1991; and Suellen O'Grady, 'What Malcolm Wants, Malcolm Gets', *Good Weekend*, 3 September 1998.
8 Cited in Annabel Crabb, 'Stop at Nothing: The Life and Adventures of Malcolm Turnbull', *Quarterly Essay*, issue 34, 2009, pp. 17, 19.
9 See, for example, Stan Anson's psychobiography of Bob Hawke: *Hawke: An Emotional Life*, McPhee Gribble, 1992.
10 Ashley L Watts et al., 'The Double-Edged Sword of Grandiose Narcissism: Implications for Successful and Unsuccessful Leadership Among US Presidents', *Psychological Science*, vol. 24, no. 12, 2013, pp. 2739–89.
11 Graham Little, 'Zeus, Mate, Not Narcissus', *Arena Magazine*, no. 21, February–March, pp. 17–20.
12 Annabel Crabb, 'Stop at Nothing: The Life and Adventures of Malcolm Turnbull', *Quarterly Essay*, issue 34, rev. edn, 2016.
13 Godwin Grech email to Malcolm Turnbull, 7 November 2008.
14 Godwin Grech email to Malcolm Turnbull, 5 June 2009.

Two—The Bower Bird

1 See, for example, George Brandis, 'John Howard and the Australian Liberal Tradition', in Peter van Onselen (ed.), *Liberals and Power: The Road Ahead*, Melbourne University Publishing, Carlton, 2008.
2 Malcolm Turnbull, Sir Robert Menzies Lecture, Melbourne, 8 October 2009.
3 Peter van Onselen, 'Majority of Libs Oppose ETS Plan', *The Australian*, 29 September 2009.
4 Manning, ch. 14.
5 James MacGregor Burns, *Leadership*, Harper and Row, New York, 1978.
6 Peter Hartcher, 'The 28 Words That Sealed Malcolm Turnbull's Fate', *The Sydney Morning Herald*, 21 May 2016, http://www.smh.com.au/comment/the-28-words-that-have-sealed-malcolm-turnbulls-fate-20160520-gp06ks.html (viewed 21 May 2016).
7 Turnbull's personal lead over Shorten as preferred economic manager was 54–20 in Newspoll, March 2016.

Three—An Agile Start

1 Tony Abbott, *Battlelines*, Melbourne University Press, Carlton, 2009, pp. 173–6.
2 The formal merger of the Liberal and National parties in Queensland has heightened the applicability of this point.

Four—The Delcons

1 This is not necessarily a partisan view. The Australian Law Reform Commission recommended a review of the broad nature of 'offence' under this section of the Act. See Australian Law Reform Commission, *Traditional Rights and Freedoms – Encroachment by Commonwealth Laws: Final Report*, ALRC Report 129, December 2015, p. 113.
2 See David Frum, 'The Republican Revolt', *The Atlantic Monthly*, 9 September 2015, http://www.theatlantic.com/politics/archive/2015/09/the-republican-revolt/404365/ (viewed 12 September 2015).
3 Niki Savva, *The Road to Ruin: How Tony Abbott and Peta Credlin Destroyed Their Own Government*, Scribe, Brunswick, 2016.
4 While Howard was required to write Peter King a formal reference as the sitting Liberal MP, it was an incredibly perfunctory document, which Turnbull noted to close supporters at the time. Howard made his support for Turnbull's candidacy clear privately, echoing such sentiments publicly by using media interviews to reiterate Turnbull's right to challenge King despite King having served only one term.
5 Waleed Aly, 'What's Right: The Future of Conservatism in Australia', in *Quarterly Essay*, issue 37, 2010. See also Kelly S Fielding et al., 'Australian Politicians' Beliefs About Climate Change: Political Partisanship and Political Ideology', *Environmental Politics*, vol. 21, no. 5, 2012, pp. 712–33.
6 See various chapters in: Peter van Onselen (ed.), *Liberals and Power: The Road Ahead*, Melbourne University Press, Carlton, 2008.

Five—Doubling Down

1 Not quite doubling the number of senators: Northern and Australian Capital Territory senators have three-year terms only.
2 See Howard's speech to the International Democratic Union, Washington, June 2002.
3 Ian McAllister and Sarah M Cameron, *Trends in Australian Public Opinion: Results of the Australian Election Survey 1987–2013*, Australian National University, Canberra, 2014.
4 Justin Wolfers and Andrew Leigh, 'Three Tools for Forecasting Federal Elections: Lessons from 2001', *Australian Journal of Political Science*, vol. 37, issue 2, 2002, pp. 223–40.

5 Errington and van Onselen, *Battleground*, pp. 140–41.

6 Andrew Spong, 'Why Isn't Australia's Future Submarine Project Further Advanced?', Australian Defence College, Centre for Defence and Strategic Studies, Canberra, November 2015, p. 14.

7 Peter Hartcher, 'PM Malcolm Turnbull's Plan to Triumph: It's All About Investment', *The Sydney Morning Herald*, 7 May 2016, http://www.smh.com.au/federal-politics/federal-election-2016/pm-malcolm-turnbulls-plan-to-triumph-its-all-about-investment-20160506-gooet3.html (viewed 7 May 2016).

Six—Eight Weeks Is a Long Time in Politics

1 Carol Johnson, 'Labor's Populist Election Narrative Fails to Placate Business – At Its Peril', *The Conversation*, 30 May 2016, https://theconversation.com/labors-populist-election-narrative-fails-to-placate-business-at-its-peril-60053 (viewed 30 May 2016).

2 Pamela Williams, 'Federal Election 2016: Peta Credlin Made Sky No-Go Zone', *The Australian*, 5 July 2016, http://www.theaustralian.com.au/federal-election-2016/federal-election-2016-peta-credlin-made-sky-nogo-zone/news-story/f55f1156bcac03690f38e171861dbdfc (viewed 5 July 2016).

3 Mark Rolfe, 'Honour Thy Parents, Lead Thy Nation: Turnbull and Shorten Play to the Family Feeling', *The Conversation*, 8 June 2016, https://theconversation.com/honour-thy-parents-lead-thy-nation-turnbull-and-shorten-play-to-the-family-feeling-60629 (viewed 25 June 2016).

Seven—Mediscare

1 Wayne Errington and Peter van Onselen, 'Electoral Databases: Big Brother or Democracy Unbound', *Australian Journal of Political Science*, vol. 39, issue 2, 2004.

2 Paul Kelly, *The End of Certainty*, Allen & Unwin, SYDNEY 1992, p. 643.

3 Narelle Miragliotta and Wayne Errington, 'Legislative Recruitment and Models of Party Organisation: Evidence from Australia', *Journal of Legislative Studies*, vol. 18, no. 2, 2012, pp. 21–40.

Eight—You Had One Job

1 Renata Bongiorno, 'Coalition's Lost Ground on Women MPs Shows We Need to Tackle New Gender Biases', *The Conversation*, 12 July 2016, https://theconversation.com/coalitions-lost-ground-on-women-mps-shows-we-need-to-tackle-new-gender-biases-62220 (accessed 12 July 2016).

ACKNOWLEDGEMENTS

We couldn't have produced this book just two months after the election without the miracle workers at MUP: Sally Heath, Nikki Lusk, Cathy Smith, Perri Palmieri and Louise Adler.

Thanks also to researchers Brendan McAffrie and Kim Sorensen. David Adams provided invaluable advice on the vexed issue of political psychology.

Peter would like to thank his wife Ainslie for her support, and dedicates his contribution in this book to his daughters, Sasha and Chloe.

Wayne would like to thank Peter.

INDEX